**Matthieu
PINON**

THE TOKYO TOURIST SURVIVAL GUIDE

The Ultimate Companion to Japan's Capital City

INSIGHT
EDITIONS

SAN RAFAEL · LOS ANGELES · LONDON

INSIGHT
EDITIONS

PO Box 3088
San Rafael, CA 94912
www.insighteditions.com

Find us on Facebook: www.facebook.com/InsightEditions
Follow us on Instagram: @insighteditions

All rights reserved. Published by Insight Editions, San Rafael, California, in 2026.

© YNNIS EDITIONS
Originally published by Ynnis, France, in 2022 under the title of *Manuel de survie du touriste à Tokyo*. All rights reserved

English translation by Andie Ho.
English translation © 2026 Insight Editions.

No part of this book may be reproduced in any form without written permission from the publisher.

ISBN: 979-8-3374-0441-7

Publisher: Raoul Goff
SVP, Co-Publisher: Vanessa Lopez
VP, Manufacturing: Alix Nicholaeff
Art Director: Matt Girard
Designer: Kayleigh Hutcheson
Senior Editor: Stephen Fall
Editorial Assistant: Xander Guidry
Executive Managing Editor: Maria Spano
Managing Editorial Assistant: Lindsay Gibson
Senior Production Manager: Greg Steffen
Strategic Production Planner: Lina s Palma-Temena

ROOTS of PEACE   REPLANTED PAPER

Insight Editions, in association with Roots of Peace, will plant two trees for each tree used in the manufacturing of this book. Roots of Peace is an internationally renowned humanitarian organization dedicated to eradicating land mines worldwide and converting war-torn lands into productive farms and wildlife habitats. Roots of Peace will plant two million fruit and nut trees in Afghanistan and provide farmers there with the skills and support necessary for sustainable land use.

Manufactured in China by Insight Editions

10 9 8 7 6 5 4 3 2 1

YNNIS

President: Cedric Littardi
Editorial Director: Sébastien Rost
French Edition: Philippe Vallotti
Editing: Sarah Touzeau and Mélissa Veludo
Cover: Sébastien Rost
Graphic Design and Mock-Up: Wilfid Desachy
Ideogram Research: Jeanne Bucher
Communications and Marketing: Camille Nogueira
Coordination: Jeanne Bucher
English Translation: Andie Ho
Special thanks to Zackary Amara and Stéphanie Ah-Fa

The images featured on these pages are published solely to illustrate the authors' content and are all © of their owners.

Ynnis Éditions
38 rue Notre-Dame-De-Nazareth
75003 Paris, France
www.ynnis-editions.fr
Instagram: @ynnis_editions
Facebook: Ynnis Éditions
X: @YnnisEditions

CONTENTS

INTRODUCTION

I travel to Japan frequently for work, specifically to Tokyo. The first time I set foot in Japan, there were no smartphones or 4G to guide me through the labyrinthian megacity and its indecipherable language. I had nothing to lean on but a crumpled map of the city, a phone card, and a network of expat friends to get me through my visit to the enigmatic city.

As the years went by, the telephone booths that used to dot the cityscape began to disappear, overtaken by a pocket-size device that I could use anywhere and anytime to answer my questions. Even so, I continued picking up tidbits from friends and colleagues, who taught me local and regional customs and tips and tricks to make my stays more comfortable. I learned a whole array of information I wish I'd known on my first trip when I was lost in the mazelike subway system or befuddled by a restaurant menu.

I've chosen to share my bag of tricks with you to facilitate your own trip to Tokyo. Whether you're there to check out the traditional culture, food scene, architecture, pop culture, or sporting events, this book offers practical advice for each step of the way. All this advice is designed to:

- Save you time
- Save you money
- Help you communicate
- Get you through the inevitable hiccups
- Help you understand local etiquette
- Anticipate obstacles that might disrupt your trip

That is why this book is called *The Tokyo Tourist Survival Guide.* This collection of handy information isn't a traditional travel guide, for several reasons. First, there are already countless travel guides out there, many of them truly excellent. You might even have already purchased one for your trip—a perfect complement to this book.

Second, Tokyo is constantly evolving. Businesses move or close. Travel guides have to be updated regularly or else they become obsolete. Furthermore, despite my many travels to Tokyo, I haven't even come close to seeing the entire city, and there are many exciting places I haven't seen. That's why travel guides are usually group efforts. It takes a whole team to cover everything!

Finally, and most importantly in my opinion, this book is designed to help you travel alone. Whatever your destination, this book tells you how to get there. Whatever local specialty you hope to try, it will help you order it. This guide offers recommendations for any interest and regardless of whether you're traveling alone or with friends or family. Like a genie in a lamp, *The Tokyo Tourist Survival Guide* is here to make *your* wishes come true. You can customize your own trip instead of following a predetermined itinerary.

HOW TO READ
THIS BOOK

The Tokyo Tourist Survival Guide is designed to answer your questions, right when you need it most. That means it has to be faster and more efficient to use than a search engine—a tall order! To achieve this, I worked closely with the publishing team to structure the book so that you can find the information you need in seconds.

Each chapter (Getting Around, Day-to-Day, Dining, Things to Do, Entertainment, Minor Emergencies) is dedicated to an essential aspect of traveling and opens with a table of contents. Simply find the topic you need and flip to the correct page, then skim the headings to find what you're looking for.

If you're trying to communicate with someone, the last section in each chapter contains relevant words and phrases in Japanese. You can either read the words phonetically or point to the Japanese characters. Blank pages are provided for you to write in if necessary.

Of course, you can also read this book cover to cover, perhaps in preparation for your trip and possibly alongside a traditional travel guide. This will help you avoid certain difficulties, even if you don't remember everything. But you don't have to, since you can carry *The Tokyo Tourist Survival Guide* with you at all times!

Finally, you may choose to read this book simply for a practical take on Japanese traditions and customs. But be warned: Once you've finished, you'll feel the urge to go to Tokyo to check it out for yourself.

PROLOGUE

WHAT TO KNOW ABOUT TOKYO
BEFORE YOU GO

Credit: Tokyoship

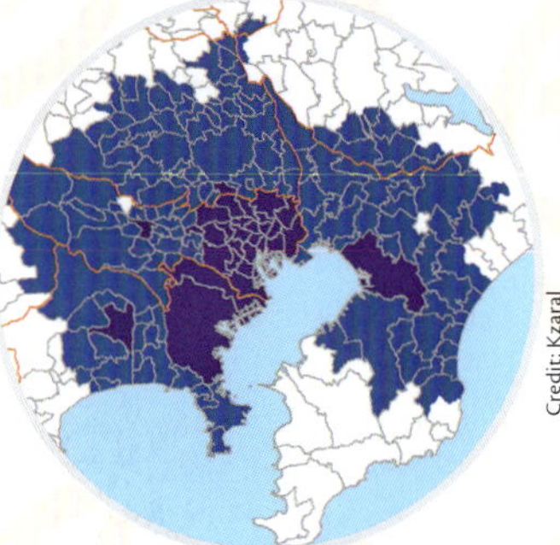

Credit: Kzaral

Credit: Kzaral

TOKYO IS NOT JUST **ONE CITY**

In 1943, Tokyo was legally changed from a city to one of 47 prefectures in Japan. Since then, it has sprawled beyond its original borders into neighboring prefectures to become the world's largest megacity. Depending on the context, Tokyo can refer to:

- The 23 special wards that formed the original city (population 10 million), each governed by its own mayor.

- The prefecture of Tokyo, which includes 30 or so additional communities to the west of the 23 wards, each headed by a governor.

- The city of Tokyo, which has a radius of over 35 miles and encompasses six neighboring prefectures and has a population of 37 million.

By comparison, the New York metropolitan area has a population of around 20 million, with around eight million in New York City proper.

DONUT CITY

New York City is often described as a grid for its crosshatched streets, Paris as a snail for the spiral placement of its *arrondissements*. Central Tokyo, however, is laid out in concentric rings, somewhat like a donut. At the donut hole lies the Imperial Palace, closed to mere mortals as are parts of its gardens. The circular Yamanote line (see p. 30) forms the border.

Credit: Miki Yoshihito

THE **SAFEST CITY** IN THE WORLD

You can rest easy traveling to Tokyo, which has the lowest crime rate in the world. You don't have to worry about being mugged or attacked. And if you lose a valuable, the chances of finding it are over 90% (see p. 33)!

Even the architecture is safe. Because Tokyo experiences frequent earthquakes, the city has stringent earthquake safety standards! For instance, you'll notice that buildings are placed at least a few centimeters apart. Nevertheless, most earthquakes are so minor that you can't even feel them if you're on the train.

JAPANESE
STEREOTYPES

Despite a certain familiarity with Japan, Americans still have certain stereotypes about the culture—some of which are based in truth. Take the quiz yourself!

JAPANESE PEOPLE ONLY EAT SUSHI

TRUE ☐ FALSE ☑

Although conveyor belt sushi establishments have brought sushi to the masses, it is still considered a luxury in Japan, to be eaten mostly on special occasions (birthdays, graduations, sports wins). In reality, Japanese cuisine is exceptionally diverse, as is evidenced by Tokyo's 150,000 restaurants. By comparison, New York City has fewer than 18,000!

ALL JAPANESE PEOPLE ARE BUDDHIST

TRUE ☑ FALSE ☑

There are two main religions in Japan, with the primary one being Shinto, an ancestral animist religion that holds that the Japanese emperor is divine. Shinto practices are still in evidence in certain daily Japanese customs, which may appear superstitious to outsiders. Buddhism, on the other hand, was imported from China by aristocrats in the fifth century and gained popularity among the commonfolk as they grew more literate. As Shinto and Buddhism were each declared the national religion at some point in history, they now coexist in Tokyo, where Buddhist temples mingle with Shinto shrines.

JAPANESE PEOPLE ARE PETITE

TRUE ☑ FALSE ☐

The average Japanese male is 5'6" (compared to 5'9" in the US), whereas the average Japanese female is 5'0" (compared to 5'4" in the US). The obesity rate is 5% (versus 42% in the US), though that is changing with the rise of fast food. Something to consider if you hope to go clothes shopping (see p. 58)!

JAPANESE PEOPLE ARE POLITE AND RESPECTFUL

TRUE ☑ FALSE ☐

Etiquette is everything in Japanese society. You'll experience unfailing politeness. In return, make the effort to learn a few essential Japanese phrases. Not only is it the courteous thing to do; you may find it extremely helpful.

JAPANESE PEOPLE SPEND ALL THEIR TIME AT WORK

TRUE ☐ FALSE ☑

The Japanese may spend a lot of time at work but their hourly profitability rates are lower. As soon as they clock out, they blow off steam in the city's restaurants and bars, karaoke clubs, and video game arcades.

Japan has 16 national holidays, among the highest in the world. The country shuts down during Golden Week, a series of four holidays in late April and early May that many people turn into a full week off!

SUMO WRESTLING IS THE NATIONAL SPORT

TRUE ☑ FALSE ☑

Historically speaking, sumo wrestling is the most famous Japanese sport. But it turns out the Japanese love baseball almost as much as Americans do!

Credit: DX Broadrec

THE JAPANESE DON'T LIKE TATTOOS

TRUE ☐ FALSE ☑

Because of their association with the Japanese mafia, some establishments (public baths, gyms) ban tattoos or require you to cover them up. However, this custom is slowly eroding under government regulation and as younger generations adopt aspects of Western culture. Regardless, you won't see many Japanese people with tattoos.

JAPANESE PEOPLE DON'T SPEAK ENGLISH

TRUE ☑ FALSE ☐

Despite having a large vocabulary, Japanese people generally find English grammar difficult. And be mindful of your accent. You might be easier to understand if you speak English with a Japanese accent! Though younger generations have picked up more English through social media, you may still find it easier to simply draw pictures with pen and paper!

THE JAPANESE LANGUAGE

Don't be afraid to try your hand at Japanese. After all, the Japanese generally don't speak a lot of English. Outside of touristy areas, large commercial centers, and major train stations, no one speaks English.

This book isn't going to teach you Japanese. That's not the point. But the next few pages provide a starting point as well as a pronunciation guide.

JAPANESE 101

Japanese has five vowels:

A	I	U	E	O
hiragana	hiragana	hiragana	hiragana	hiragana

pronunciation	pronunciation	pronunciation	pronunciation	pronunciation
[ah]	[ee]	[oo]	[eh]	[oh]

If you add a consonant at the beginning, you get a series of syllables. Here are examples with K and N:

KA	KI	KU	KE	KO
hiragana	hiragana	hiragana	hiragana	hiragana

pronunciation	pronunciation	pronunciation	pronunciation	pronunciation
[kah]	[kee]	[koo]	[keh]	[koh]

NA	NI	NU	NE	NO
hiragana	hiragana	hiragana	hiragana	hiragana

pronunciation	pronunciation	pronunciation	pronunciation	pronunciation
[nah]	[nee]	[noo]	[neh]	[noh]

There are many exceptions; for example, SI is pronounced SHEE and TU is pronounced TSOO. Make sure to pronounce each syllable separately.

MAN-GA, GE-I-SHA, A-I-KI-DO, SU-SHI, KI-MO-NO, ZEN

WRITING

Japanese has FOUR writing systems:

- **Kanji.** These ideograms were imported from China. Each has its own meaning but its pronunciation varies depending on the context. There are over 6,000 of them, around 2,000 of which are used in everyday life.

Credit: Ayu Nabila

- **Hiragana and katakana.** These are phonetic scripts with a different symbol for each of the 46 essential syllables in the Japanese language (see chart in the appendix).

- **Romaji.** This is the transliteration of the Japanese language using the Latin alphabet. In this book, romaji will be the most useful in helping you communicate.

Credit: Branden Yamada

HOW TO READ **ROMAJI**

B & V / R & L

- B and V are pronounced the same (much as in certain variants of Spanish), and so are R and L.
  BI-DE-O KA-ME-LA = video camera, TE-LE-BI = television

S & Z

- S is always pronounced "ess" and never "zee." If a word has a "zee" sound, it will be written with a Z.
  MI-SO (not mi-zo), BON-SAI (not bon-zai), BAN-ZAI, KA-WA-SA-KI (not Ka-wa-za-ki), SU-ZU-KI, WA-SA-BI (not wa-za-bi)

Ø

- Gemination is like a period. It adds a slight pause in the word before continuing and accenting the following consonant. In romaji, it is written as a double consonant. However, we'll use the null sign. Gemination can completely change the meaning of a word!
  NE-KO (cat) ≠ NE-Ø-KO (root)
  KI-TE (come) ≠ KI-Ø-TE (stamp)

ENGLISH WITH A JAPANESE TWIST

- The Japanese have adopted many English words into their daily vocabulary but pronounce them their own way.
  coffee -> KO-HI, hamburger -> HAN-BA-A-GA, door -> DO-A, internet -> IN-TA-A-NE-Ø-TO, golf -> GO-RU-FU, ice cream -> A-I-SU KU-RI-MU, service -> SA-BI-SU, hot dog -> HO-Ø-TO DO-Ø-GU

- When communicating in English, instead of speaking louder, try this instead:

Use short sentences or even single keywords. "Where station?" is easier to understand than "Could you tell me where the station is?"

Use Japanese pronunciation. Instead of asking for a taxi or bus, ask for a TA-KU-SHI or BA-SU. You're not looking for a hotel, but a HO-TEH-RU.

In this book, each word or phrase is provided in kanji and kana (for locals to read) and in romaji and spelled out phonetically in English (so you can pronounce them)—along with their English translations, of course.

TEN WORDS YOU SHOULD KNOW

SUMIMASEN
(soo-mee-ma-sen)

Excuse me

ARIGATŌ GOZAIMASU
(ah-lee-ga-toh go-za-ee-mass)

Thank you

ONEGAISHIMASU
(oh-neh-ga-ee-see-mass)

Please

OHAYŌ GOZAIMASU
(oh-ha-yo go-za-ee-mass)

Good morning

KONNICHIWA
(koh-nee-chee-wa)

Good afternoon

HAI
(ha-ee)

Yes

IIE
(ee-yeh)

No

WAKARIMASEN
(wa-kar-ee-mass-sen)

I don't understand

GOMEN NASAI
(go-men nah-sy)

Sorry, please excuse me (used to apologize for an error or faux pas)

DAIJŌBU
(da-ee-jo-boo)

I'm fine, I'm all set, no thanks

BEFORE YOU GO

With a bit of planning, you can make life easier for yourself upon arriving in Japan. Here is a brief overview of things to consider before you take off.

PASSPORT

This might sound like a no-brainer, but make sure your passport is valid for the duration of your stay! You should always carry it with you in Japan, if only for the tax exemptions that many stores offer to tourists.

If you need to apply for or renew your passport, make sure to do so several months before your departure date. Check out the US State Department website for more information.

Also, keep a photocopy of your passport stashed somewhere. It will make it easier to replace if you lose it.

PLANNING YOUR STAY

Plan out your activities in advance. It's best to group them by geographical area. While the mass transit system is efficient and ubiquitous in Tokyo, it can also be time-consuming to travel from point A to point B.

For the first few days after you arrive, keep near the Yamanote train stations (in the Shibuya/Harajuku, Ueno, and Ikebukuro districts) to help you become familiar with the transit system. Once you feel comfortable, you can venture out farther to places such as Odaiba, Yokohama, or the Studio Ghibli museum.

CURRENCY

Contact your bank and ask them to raise your weekly or monthly ATM withdrawal limit. You may need to withdraw large sums of cash while traveling, and you don't want to find yourself unable to do so when the money is in the account!

Ask your bank about fees for foreign ATM withdrawals and credit card transactions. If you plan ahead, you can even open an account with an online bank with lower fees.

Make sure to buy a fair amount of Japanese currency (yen) before you leave. Track the dollar-to-yen exchange rate to buy at the best time, and remember to compare exchange rates at different financial institutions. Some charge fees for buying currency with a credit card, so you may want to pay in cash.

TRAVELING BY TRAIN

A JR Pass lets you travel for free on Japan Railways lines for seven, 14, or 21 days. This won't be useful to you if you'll only be visiting Tokyo, but if you plan on traveling from Tokyo to the western part of Japan (Osaka, Kyoto, Hiroshima), a single round trip on a major line may pay for the pass itself. You can choose when to activate the pass, preferably as you leave Tokyo. Choose a pass based on how long you'll be exploring outside Tokyo, not the length of your stay in Japan as a whole.

You cannot buy a JR Pass in Japan! They must be preordered online (make sure to compare prices at different websites) or via an agency. Children ages six to 11 receive a discount, and kids under six travel free. You'll receive vouchers that you can exchange for passes at major stations in Tokyo.

You can buy a JR Pass online. There are several websites certified by the JR company, so make sure to shop around. Alternatively, you can book them through a travel agency.

FLIGHTS TO **TOKYO**

Other than the cost, there are two major considerations when booking a flight: the number of bags you plan to check and the airport you fly into. Most major airlines have a weight limit of 50 pounds per bag, though this can vary, and the cost of checking bags also depends on the airline and any perks you might be entitled to. If you can, fly into Haneda Airport (also known as Tokyo International Airport) rather than Narita International Airport. It's closer to Tokyo.

The time difference between Tokyo and mainland USA ranges from 13 to 17 hours ahead, depending on your home time zone and daylight savings time. To minimize jet lag, try to sleep on the flight if you'll be arriving in the morning or stay awake if you'll be landing later in the day. You'll have anywhere from 10 to 14 hours, plus layover time, to adjust.

Credit: Kentaro Iemoto

FLIGHTS WITHIN **JAPAN**

If you want to visit other parts of Japan, particularly cities far from Tokyo (Hokkaido, Okinawa, Kagoshima), check out ANA and JAL, two major national airlines that offer special rates for tourists. Your international flight to Japan doesn't have to be with either of them to receive the discount. One of the special deals is for flights at a fixed price (¥7,700 or ¥11,000), which you can book before you leave home or once you arrive in Japan, up to 24 hours before departure.

Each airline has its own website for its special deals:

JAL
www.jal.co.jp/ar/en/

If you're nervous about booking it yourself, visit a JAL or ANA office or travel agency and book the special fare at the same time as your flight to Tokyo.

FINDING **RECOMMENDATIONS**

If you're traveling to Japan, you probably have certain can't-miss experiences in mind, from the food scene to traditional Japanese culture to the technology, martial arts customs, or pop culture. Find the places you know you'll want to visit, draw up your schedule and travel plans accordingly, and make your reservations. The three best sources of information are:

Internet: If you can't read Japanese, you'll miss out on a lot of information.

Travel guides: Buy the latest edition to ensure the information is up to date.

Japan National Tourism Organization (JNTO) or travel agencies.

If you have friends who have been to Japan, ask them for recommendations and make a list.

TRAVELING **BY CAR**

https://english.jaf.or.jp/

If you want to travel by car, you must get your driver's license translated by the Japan Automobile Federation (JAF). It costs ¥3,000 and takes some time.

JAF Tokyo office:

2-2-17 Shiba, Minato-ku, Tokyo 105-8562

Japanese traffic customs are different from the USA, not least of which is driving on the left side of the road! Learn the meanings of various Japanese signs and signals before you leave.

LODGING

In June 2018, a highly restrictive law was passed that reduced the number of Airbnb rooms on the market by 80%. So make sure to start your lodging research months in advance! In general, Airbnb isn't a very good option, unless you're bent on renting a private apartment at any cost (literally)—for instance, if you're traveling with a large group.

Ryokan are traditional inns that offer a relaxing getaway. You can almost forget you're in a major city. But ryokan are few and far between and you have to reserve at least six months in advance, especially if you'll be in Tokyo in the spring (April to May) or summer (July to August), the two busy tourist seasons.

For younger travelers more concerned with budget over luxuries, Tokyo has plenty of guesthouses and youth hostels offering shared rooms. Your belongings will be safe, but expect minimal, even Spartan, amenities.

If you find a suspiciously inexpensive hotel on a booking website, check whether it's a capsule hotel or pod hotel. These tiny, bed-size pods are intended as places for office workers to crash for a night and are typically not suitable for longer stays or for tourists.

ELECTRONICS

Japan uses the 100V standard, as opposed to North America's 120V. Most modern phones and laptops can handle a range of voltages. Check the label on your charger. If you do need a different power cord, you can buy one or bring your own and purchase a voltage converter when you arrive.

For USB-powered devices, inexpensive wall chargers are readily available in Japan, so you can leave yours at home. In any case, your Pocket Wi-Fi should come with a USB charger.

Pack a power bank (battery pack) if you have one. If you don't, you should invest in one as soon as you arrive (see p. 132).

Pack electronic devices in your carry-on bags for the flight to Tokyo to guard against damage or theft.

A TASTE OF **AMERICA**

If you'll be spending time with locals (an Airbnb host, tour guide, host family, friend), bring some goodies from home as a gift. The Japanese have a custom of omiyage (oh-mee-ah-gay) or bringing back small gifts after a journey. Some good ideas are boxes of chocolate, candies, or treats in brands that aren't available in Japan.

INTERNET / APPS

Internet access is essential in a technology-centric country like Japan, and yet free Wi-Fi is hard to find, despite claims to the contrary. You'll want to rent a pocket Wi-Fi device, a portable high-speed modem that you can share with your travel companions. You can reserve one in advance and pick it up at the post office inside the airport simply by showing your passport.

You can also buy a SIM card to use in your phone once you arrive in Japan. On one hand, you won't have to worry about battery life, unlike with pocket Wi-Fi. On the other hand, you won't be able to share your connection or use your favorite messaging apps (WhatsApp, LINE, WeChat, etc.).

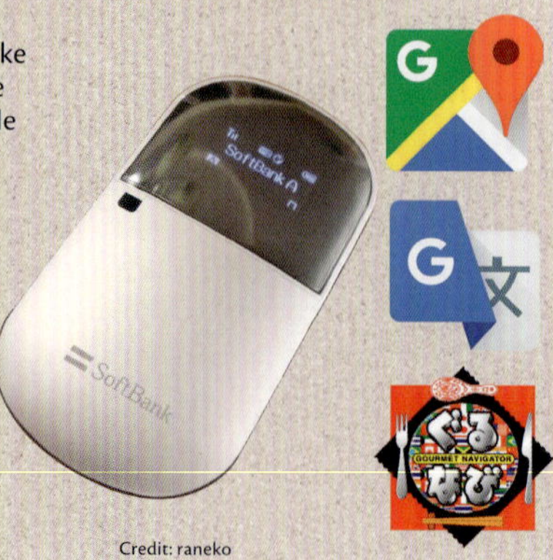

Credit: raneko

Google Maps and Google Translate are two apps that will be particularly useful to you. Some close seconds are GuruNavi, which displays restaurants near you, and HappyCow, a restaurant app that displays vegan eateries.

Make sure to disable roaming to avoid nasty surprises on your phone bill when you get home!

MEDICATION / TOILETRIES

If you take medications, make sure you have enough to last you the duration of your stay. If you'll be staying longer than a month, you'll need permission from the Yakkan Shoumei, the Japanese ministry of health, to bring in medicines for personal use. Visit the website below to apply for permission. Allow at least a month to receive approval.

www.mhlw.go.jp/english/policy/health-medical/pharmaceuticals/01.html

Tampons are nearly impossible to find in Japan. Be sure to bring some with you.

You'll also want to bring two-ply tissues, which don't exist in Japan.

Also, remember your toothbrush. Japanese toothbrush heads are tiny compared to ours!

For men, you may want to bring non-electric razors to avoid dealing with voltage differences. For women, you'll want to bring your own razors or hair removal wax, as most Japanese women prefer to use laser removal or intense pulsed light technology.

Finally, if you're planning to get frisky, bring your own condoms. Not all Japanese condoms are made to protect against sexually transmitted infections.

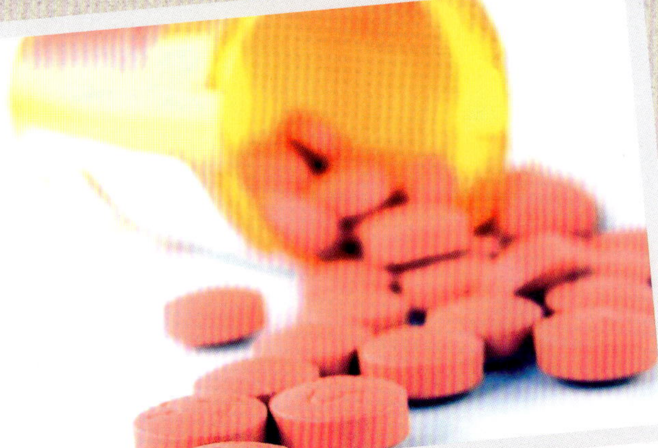

CLOTHING

See p. 108 to 111 for clothing recommendations for each season.

Bring shoes that are easy to take off and put on (leave the combat boots at home).

TIP!
For young children, choose shoes with Velcro straps.

NOTE!
Make sure your socks don't have holes!

TIP!
Make a list of everything you pack. That way you can check to make sure you don't leave anything behind when you pack to return home.

RESERVATIONS

The Japanese are planners. They like to book tickets in advance. If you don't do the same, you may arrive at that restaurant, museum, or event to find that it sold out months ago. Decide on the highlights of your trip and make reservations as soon as possible. For assistance or recommendations, contact the Japan National Tourism Organization (JNTO).

Website: www.japan.travel/en/us
Telephone:
  Los Angeles: (213) 623-1952
  New York City: (212) 757-5640

USEFUL **WORDS**

COUNTING IN JAPANESE

Counting in Japanese is easy.

0	1	2	3	4	5	6	7	8	9
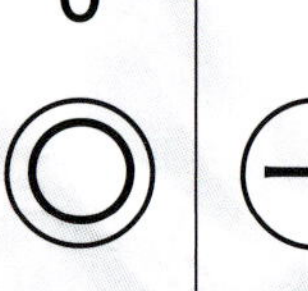	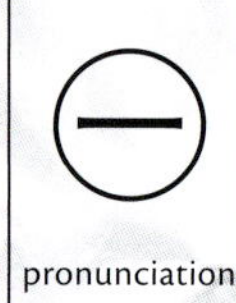	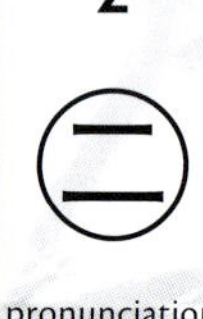	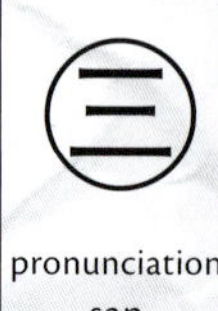		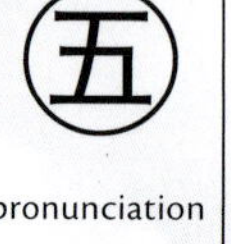		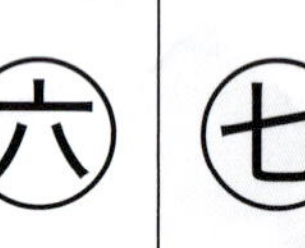		
pronunciation	pronunciation	pronunciation	pronunciation	pronunciation	pronunciation	pronunciation	pronunciation	pronunciation	pronunciation
zero [zero]	ichi [ee-chee]	ni [nee]	san [sahn]	yon [yon]	go [go]	roku [lo-koo]	nana [nah-nah]	hachi [ha-chee]	kyū [kee-oo-oo]

MULTIPLIERS

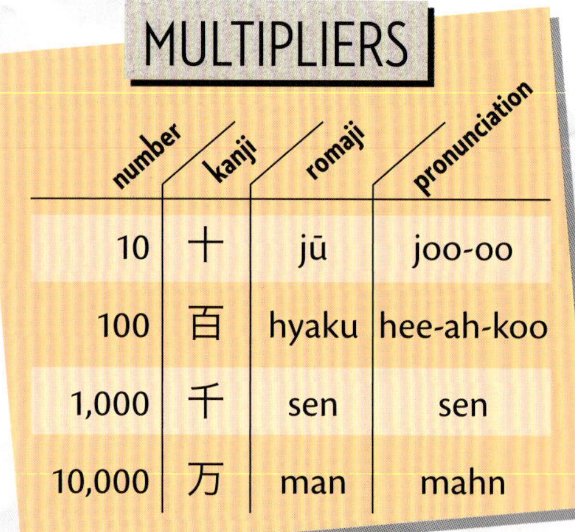

number	kanji	romaji	pronunciation
10	十	jū	joo-oo
100	百	hyaku	hee-ah-koo
1,000	千	sen	sen
10,000	万	man	mahn

To count in Japanese, place the multiplier after the corresponding number.

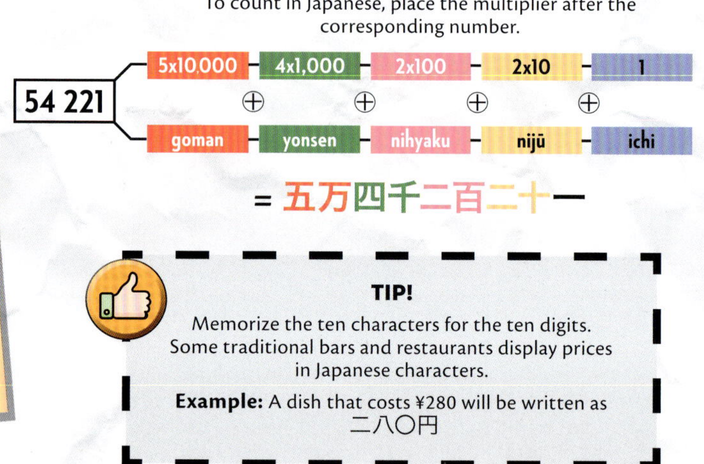

TIP!

Memorize the ten characters for the ten digits. Some traditional bars and restaurants display prices in Japanese characters.

Example: A dish that costs ¥280 will be written as
二八〇円

DATES AND **TIMES**

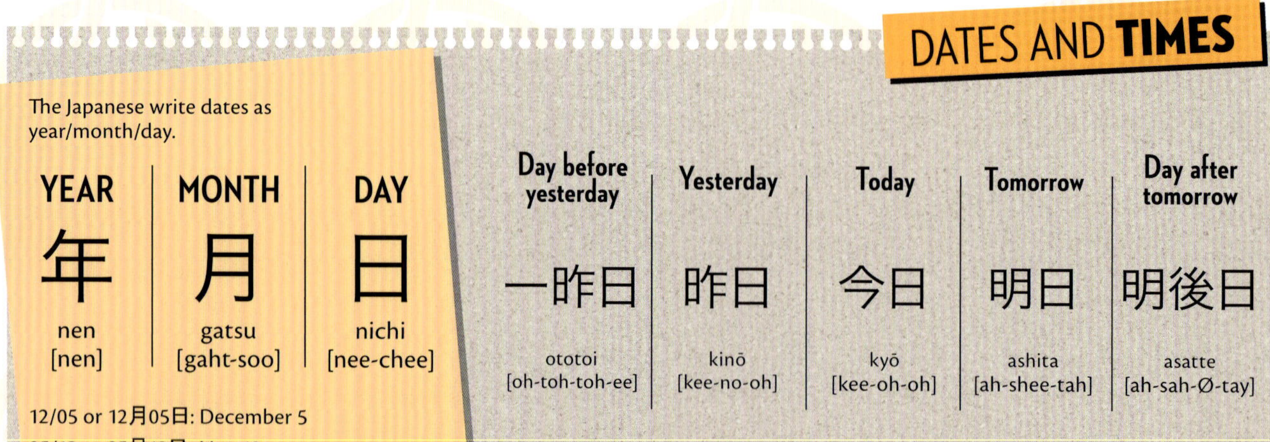

The Japanese write dates as year/month/day.

YEAR	MONTH	DAY	Day before yesterday	Yesterday	Today	Tomorrow	Day after tomorrow
年	月	日	一昨日	昨日	今日	明日	明後日
nen [nen]	gatsu [gaht-soo]	nichi [nee-chee]	ototoi [oh-toh-toh-ee]	kinō [kee-no-oh]	kyō [kee-oh-oh]	ashita [ah-shee-tah]	asatte [ah-sah-Ø-tay]

12/05 or 12月05日: December 5
05/12 or 05月12日: May 12

COLORS 色 IRO

WHITE	BLACK	RED	BLUE	YELLOW	GREEN
白	黒	赤	青	黄色	緑
shiro [shee-ro]	kuro [koo-ro]	aka [ah-kah]	ao [ah-oh]	kiiro [kee-ee-ro]	midori [mee-doh-ree]

ORANGE	PURPLE	PINK	BROWN	GOLD	SILVER
オレンジ	紫	ピンク	茶色	金色	銀色
orenji [oh-len-jee]	murasaki [moo-rah-sah-ki]	pinku [peen-koo]	cha-iro [cha-ee-lo]	kin-iro [kee-nee-lo]	gin-iro [gee-nee-lo]

INTRODUCING YOURSELF

English My name is __________________. I am American. I am ________ years old.

Characters 私の名前は ________________ です. 私はアメリカ人です. __ 歳です.

Romaji Watashi no namae wa ___________ desu. Amerikajin desu. ___ sai desu.

Pronunciation Wah-tah-shee no nah-mah-ay wah _____________ dess. Ah-meh-ri-kah-jin dess. ___ sy dess.

Early morning	Morning	Afternoon	Evening	Night
朝	午前	午後	晩	夜
asa [ah-sah]	gozen [go-zen]	gogo [goh-goh]	ban [bahn]	yoru [yoo-loo]

HOUR	MINUTE
時	分
ji [jee]	fun/pun [foon/poon]

TIP!
If you want to book something for a specific date, write down the date on a piece of paper for the booking agent to prevent confusion.

GETTING AROUND

NARITA **VS.** HANEDA

Welcome to Japan! You've picked up your checked bags at the carousel, made it through customs, and now you're on Japanese soil. How you get to Tokyo depends on which airport you flew into. But regardless of whether you're at Haneda or Narita, you'll want to follow the next few steps before heading off to your hotel.

POCKET WI-FI / SIM CARD

If you've followed the recommendations on p. 14, you'll have reserved a pocket Wi-Fi device or SIM card before you left. Your item will be waiting at the airport post office, identified by this logo.

Haneda: International arrivals arrive at Terminal 3, but the post office is located in Terminal 1 on level 1F. You can take a free monorail shuttle to get there (inquire at any information desk). Hours: 9 a.m.–5 p.m.

Narita: In Terminal 1, the post office is on level 4F. In Terminal 2, it is on level 3F. Hours: 8:30 a.m.–8 p.m. for both locations.

Credit: Nanashinodensyaku

Post office

郵便局

yuubinkyoku
[yoo-oo-been-kee-oh-koo]

TIP!

Don't worry if you didn't reserve a device ahead of time. You can still choose from a range of providers and rates.

LUGGAGE DELIVERY

Japan is one of the few countries to offer takkyūbin, also spelled TA-Q-BIN, a luggage delivery service offered by Yamato Transport, nicknamed Kuroneko [koo-roh-nay-koh]. Simply fill out a delivery form with your hotel's address and your bags will be delivered by the next morning! It costs about ¥2,000 to ¥5,000 per bag, well worth it for the freedom if you're traveling with kids.

宅急便: takkyūbin [tak-kee-oo-oo-been]

You can spot the desk easily by its logo featuring a black cat (kuro neko) carrying a kitten in its mouth.

Haneda: Note: The Kuroneko Yamato desks are easy to find in the domestic terminals (Terminals 1 and 2), but there isn't one in the international terminal. But never fear: You can request the service at the JAL ABC counter on level 2F (where you can also rent pocket Wi-Fi devices and SIM cards).

Narita: Regardless of which terminal you fly into, the Kuroneko Yamato desk is located on level 1F right past customs.

Credit: 円周率3パーセント

TRANSIT PASSES

If you'll be traveling outside of Tokyo and purchased a JR Pass in advance, now is the time to pick it up at a JR desk. If you didn't reserve one, you'll still want to swing by for help from the English-speaking staff, who will make your life easier.

Pick up your JR Pass by showing your voucher. Fill out the information requested (name, nationality, passport number) and the date you want to activate your pass. Then all you need is a signature and a stamp.

You may also want to obtain a physical IC Card or tourist card (see below for details), especially if traveling as a family, since kids ages six to 11 ride for half price but must possess an actual card.

JR EAST TRAVEL SERVICE CENTER

Haneda

Exit the terminal and head straight, then turn left near the turnstiles to the monorail.

Hours: 6:45 a.m.–8 p.m.

Narita

Regardless of which terminal you fly into, head to the JR office one level down from the ground floor (level B1), near the turnstiles for the shuttles.

Hours: Terminal 1: 8:15 a.m.–7 p.m.

Terminals 2 and 3: 8:15 a.m.–8 p.m.

Credit: TC411-507
Credit: Linearcity

NOTE!

Some desks may experience long wait times during busy periods, up to 30 minutes. Skip the lines and purchase your IC Card from a machine and pick up your JR Pass later at one of the major Tokyo train stations listed on your voucher.

HANEDA TO TOKYO

TRAIN

Pros: Frequent, precise, inexpensive.

Cons: Requires transfers.

Monorail
(free with a JR Pass)

With its panoramic view, the monorail is the best way to immerse yourself in the ambience of Tokyo. Trains leave every four minutes and arrive at Hamamatsuchō in 15 minutes.

Keikyū Line
(JR Pass not accepted)

The Keikyū Line is slightly less expensive and takes you to Shinagawa, two stations west of Hamamatsuchō (see p. 31). Make sure you take the train heading in the correct direction. Some of them go as far as Yokohama way down south!

BUS

Limousine Bus

Pros: Takes you directly to the station closest to your hotel.

Cons: May get caught in traffic, more expensive than the train.

This option is ideal for families not using the takkyūbin luggage delivery service.

TAXI

Pros: Takes you directly to your hotel.

Cons: Extremely expensive.

NARITA TO TOKYO

TRAIN

Skyliner

Pros: Fastest method.

Cons: Only serves the northeast.

The Skyliner takes you to Nippori in 35 minutes and Ueno in 40 minutes (see p. 30). You can transfer at Yamanote to reach certain stations faster and cheaper than on competing train lines.

Narita Express

Pros: Free with a JR Pass, serves the south and west.

Cons: Slow, expensive without a JR Pass.

If your hotel is in the south part of Tokyo, you'll want to get off at Shinagawa, which takes one hour. The line continues on to Shibuya, Shinjuku, and Ikebukuro (see pp. 30–31).

Keisei

Pros: Inexpensive.

Cons: Slow, not ideal if you have luggage, a regular train line.

Takes you to Nippori in an hour and 10 minutes.

Sōbu Kaisoku

Pros: Inexpensive.

Cons: Slow, not ideal if you have luggage, a regular train line.

Takes you to Tokyo station in an hour and a half (see p. 30).

TAXI

Pros: Drops you off at the door of your hotel.

Cons: Extremely expensive ($200 or more).

BUS

Limousine Bus

Pros: Comfortable, drops you off near your hotel.

Cons: Subject to traffic.

IC CARDS

IC Cards [eye-see kah-doh] serve as both a transit pass and a sort of debit card. They completely transformed the lives of Tokyoites when they were introduced in 2011. A tourist version was made available in 2019.

CHOOSING A CARD

JR and Tokyo Metro are each private companies with their own transit card: Suica for JR and Pasmo for Tokyo Metro. While the standard versions are the same, the Welcome Suica and Pasmo Passport versions differ in a few ways.

COST

Pasmo Passport: Requires a ¥500 deposit, so if you pay ¥2,000, you'll receive a card with a ¥1,500 balance.

Welcome Suica: Free. The full ¥2,000 will be loaded directly to your card.

EXPIRATION

Both cards expire 28 days after activation. Any remaining balance on the card is nonrefundable, so try to use it down to the last yen before heading home.

MAXIMUM BALANCE

The maximum amount you can load onto an IC Card is ¥20,000.

USING THE CARD

In the subway station, scan your card at the turnstile. A screen displays your balance (fares are deducted when you exit the subway station).

Konbini (convenience stores), mini-marts, and vending machines offer rectangular card readers where you tap your card to pay.

WHERE TO BUY AND RELOAD

Welcome Suica: At Haneda and Narita airports and at major JR stations in Tokyo.

Pasmo Passport:

Narita Airport: At the Keisei desk near the entrance to the Skyliner.

Haneda Airport (Terminal 1): At the Keikyū Tourist Information Center near the entrance to the Keikyū Line.

At major Tokyo Metro stations in Tokyo.

Reloading your card at vending machines

Press "English" in the upper right corner.
Select "Charge."
Insert your card into the slot provided.
Select the amount you wish to add.
Insert bills into the slot on the right.
Retrieve your card and change.

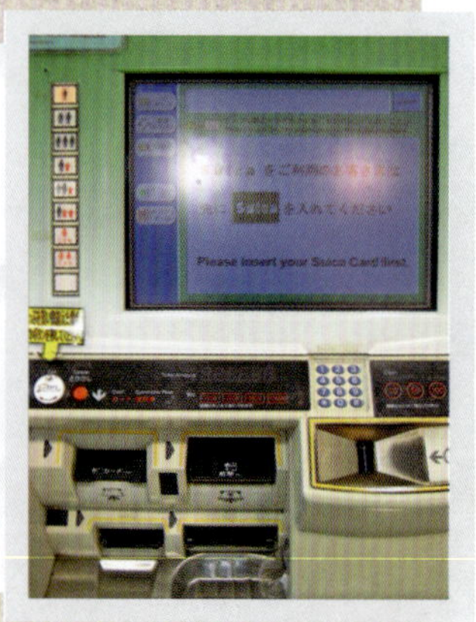

Credit: Luis Villa del Campo

STANDARD CARDS

If you'll be staying longer than 28 days, you should invest in a standard IC Card. You can also buy one for shorter stays instead of the tourist version. For both cards you'll have to pay a ¥500 deposit.

There's only one major difference besides the company issuing them: The Suica card is compatible with the iPhone's Wallet app, while the Pasmo card is not.

Standard cards expire 10 days after their last use. You can return them at any ticket window before you return home and collect any remaining balance on the card, as well as (a portion of) the deposit.

Standard cards are sold at all stations, ticket windows, and vending machines.

Buying cards at vending machines

Press "English" in the upper right corner.

Select "Purchase new Suica," then "Suica new purchase."

Press the pink Pasmo logo in the lower left, press PASMO, then press Blank Pasmo (or General User Pasmo, on older machines).

Select the amount you wish to add. Insert bills into the slot on the right. Retrieve your card and change.

SUICA FOR IPHONE

You can transfer your Suica card to your iPhone:

Open the Wallet app.

Select "Add a card."

Select "Suica transit card."

Enter the last four digits of the card and your date of birth.

Hold your phone over the card for a moment and wait for the data to transfer.

That's it! Your card has been added.

You can now toss your card (or keep it as a souvenir) and use your iPhone as your card in the subway or at konbini. Bonus: The ¥500 deposit will also be added to your virtual wallet!

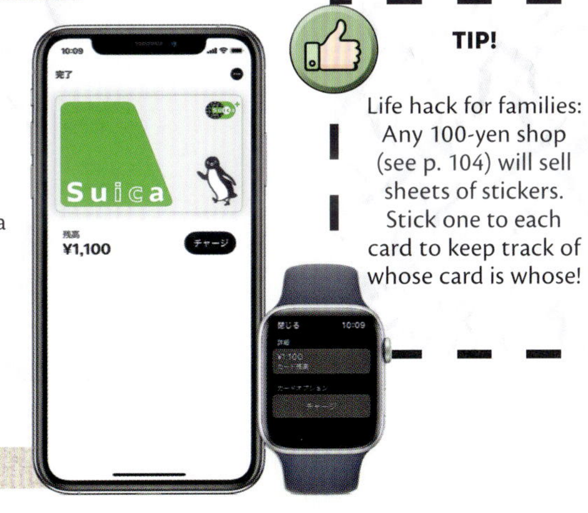

TIP!

Life hack for families: Any 100-yen shop (see p. 104) will sell sheets of stickers. Stick one to each card to keep track of whose card is whose!

RETURNING YOUR CARD

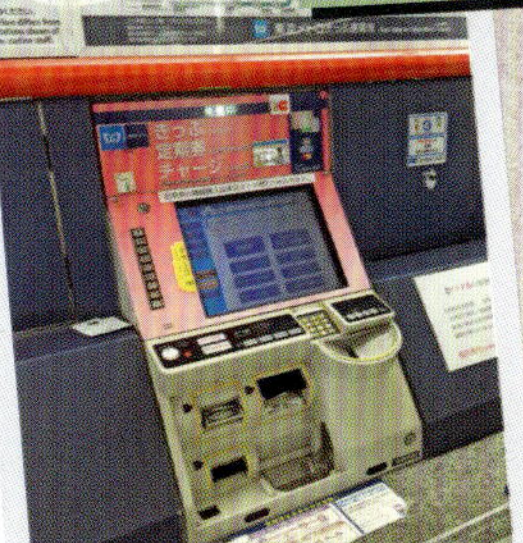

Suica cards can be returned at JR stations, and Pasmo cards can be returned at Tokyo Metro stations.

TIP!

Both kinds of cards can be returned at the airport.

Pasmo: Your remaining balance and ¥500 deposit will be refunded to you.

Suica: Your remaining balance and ¥500 deposit will be refunded to you, minus a ¥220 administrative fee. If your balance is below ¥220, you won't have to pay the difference.

CARD RANKINGS

PASMO 

SUICA

WELCOME SUICA

PASMO PASSPORT 

WHAT TO
KEEP ON YOU

PASSPORT*

Always carry your passport with you in case you get stopped by the police or simply to receive tax exemptions.

CASH

Even in Tokyo, many establishments don't take credit cards. Always carry a handful of ¥100 coins, which are useful for vending machines.

IC CARD

Essential for getting around!

POCKET WI-FI*
AND SMARTPHONE*

The internet is an essential companion. Keep an eye on your battery life.

POWER BANK

You can never be too careful.

110 V ADAPTER
-> USB + CABLE

Better safe than sorry.

Credit: Tano4595

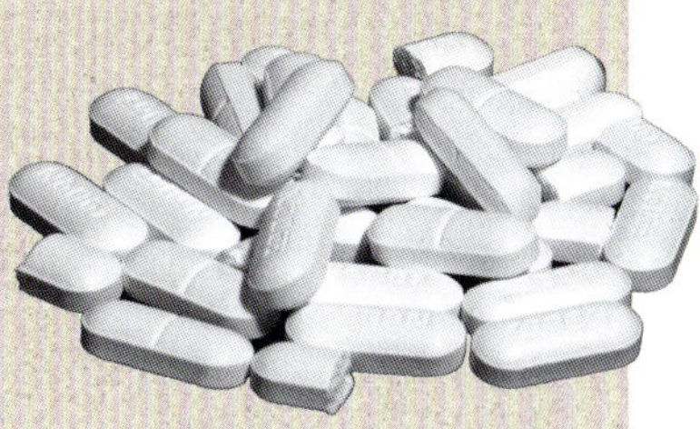

OPTIONAL

Water bottle

There are vending machines every 50 or 100 feet. But if you're going green with your own water bottle, you can refill it at any sink, including in public restrooms.

Personal medications

SPARE PLASTIC BAG

Public garbage cans are few and far between in Japan, so make sure to carry a spare plastic bag to collect your trash until you find one. They're also useful for carrying around the other plastic bags you'll inevitably accumulate with each purchase.

TOWEL

Lightweight, absorbent towels that are long and narrow, almost like a scarf, are easy to find. Rolled up (or worn around your neck), they don't take up much space and always come in handy, especially if you have kids.

PENCIL AND PAPER

Language barriers can often be overcome by drawing pictures or a map. Carry a pencil and, if possible, paper. Or turn to the Notes section of this guide for blank pages.

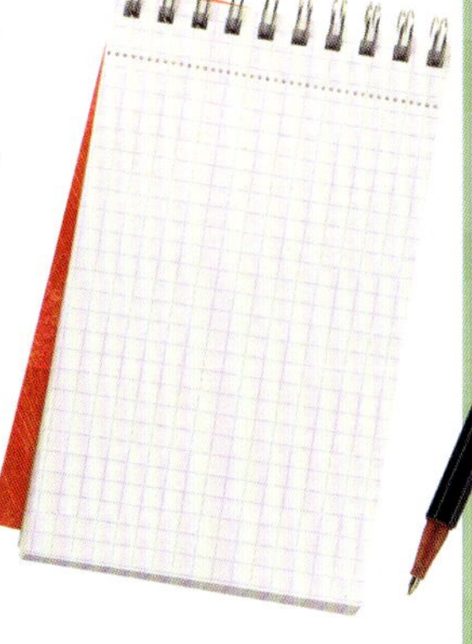

THIS GUIDE*

* Tape a business card from your hotel to the items marked with an asterisk. This will make life easier should you lose them. If you're staying at an Airbnb, write the address on a slip of paper.

TAKING THE **SUBWAY**

For a long time, the Tokyo subway was a nightmare for tourists. But the introduction of IC Cards in 2011 and the new station numbering system in 2016 has made it much easier to navigate.

THE MAJOR **COMPANIES**

Out of the dozen or so private companies that operate along Tokyo's nearly 2,000 miles of railway, three predominate:

JR-East owns most of the aboveground lines and mostly serves the outskirts of Tokyo. Its lines are always denoted by a square logo and a two-letter code, the first of which is always a J.

ACCEPTS THE JR PASS

Tokyo Metro and **Toei Subway** own nine and four underground subway lines, respectively, in central Tokyo. Both companies' lines are always identified with a colored circle with a letter.

DOES NOT ACCEPT JR PASS

PAST **YAMANOTE**

Past Yamanote, not all trains stop at all stations. The trains are named differently depending on the number of stations they stop at. If in doubt, always take the local train.

JR

Special Rapid > Commuter Express > Rapid > Local

There are also Limited Express trains that cost extra.

Other companies

Limited Express > Express > Rapid > Semi-Express/Local Express > Local

PRICING

The longer the train ride, the more it costs. To give you an idea, it costs about ¥170 for the first four stations, ¥200 for the next five, and ¥240 for the next three. Each company sets its own rates, which vary depending on several factors. In general, though, JR is slightly more expensive than its competitors.

If you switch companies during a transfer, you'll pay the cost of the first ride with the first company and then start a new ride with the next company. For instance, if you ride two stations on a JR line and two on a Toei Subway line, you'll pay ¥180 plus ¥160. It's best to try to stay with a single company as much as possible for the same ride, whether it's JR or Tokyo Metro/Toei Subway. Which one you should choose depends on a number of factors.

THE MAJOR **SUBWAY LINES**

Instead of trying to memorize the dozens of lines that crisscross the city, focus on the major lines, commonly used as landmarks on the maps outside every station. You'll almost certainly be riding them anyway during your stay.

Subway line

線

sen
[sen]

Yamanote sen 

The Yamanote sen or line is central Tokyo's unofficial border. It's easy to spot on maps outside any major station in the city, even those for non-JR lines.

> **NOTE!**
> The last trains of the night end at Ikebukuro and Ōsaki.

Chūō sen  and Chūō-Sōbu sen

These two lines are owned by JR and link the eastern and western ends of the city, cutting across the Yamanote loop. They are among the busiest lines in the city and are divided into two double tracks to ease congestion. The Chūō line is an express, connecting the Shinjuku station to the Tokyo station in 15 minutes. The Chūō-Sōbu line is a local train and takes 25 minutes to travel from Shinjuku to the Akihabara station.

Ōedo sen Ⓔ

With a slightly awkward connection between the Tochōmae and Shinjuku stations, the Ōedo line creates a loop, forming Toei Subway's answer to the Yamanote loop. If you pick up the train at either of those two stations, make sure you take the one going in the correct direction.

Ginza sen Ⓖ

The Ginza line runs roughly parallel to the Yamanote line, passing through luxury tourist districts (Ginza) and working-class neighborhoods (Asakusa).

Mita sen Ⓘ

The Mita line runs from the north to the south of Tokyo. It makes for a great landmark on Tokyo Metro maps.

SCHEDULE

The subway opens at 5 a.m. and closes starting at midnight. There are station attendants (駅員: ekiin [ay-kee-een]) at every entrance who can help you.

RUSH HOUR

- The Japanese subway passenger pushers aren't just the stuff of legend. There really are employees whose job is to pack people onto trains during rush hour. Some lines are busier than others. Avoid the hours of 7 a.m. to 9 a.m. if you possibly can, as well as 5 p.m. to 7 p.m., when commuters are heading to and from work. The most crowded line is the Tōzai sen, followed by the Odakyū sen and the Yokosuka sen.

- To accommodate the onrush of passengers, the Chūō sen and Chūō-Sōbu sen run rapid/express services during peak hours. Not only will you get caught up in the crush of people, but you might also go right past your stop.

- Try to avoid the last train of the night as well. Many of the riders squeezed into your train car may be in various states of drunkenness—always a dicey proposition.

TIP!
Don't be that person digging around for their IC Card at the turnstile. Keep it within easy reach at all times.

DETERMINING YOUR ROUTE

Method 1
Enter your starting and ending train stations into Google Maps. Different routes have different travel times and transfers.

Method 2
Inquire at the ticket window. A staff member will help you determine a route.

Method 3
Every station has a giant subway map displayed above the bank of IC Card machines. The station you're standing in will be marked in red. Find your destination on the map and the corresponding cost. Memorize where you need to transfer.

For your convenience, the maps in the Appendix are labeled with each station's code.

Example: It's easier to remember "Start at A14, transfer at A13/T10, arrive at T09" than "Start at Asakusabashi, transfer at Nihombashi, arrive at Otemachi."

Credit: Kzaral

GETTING TO THE TRAIN

Find your line (JR Lines are labeled with a colored square and a two-letter code, while Tokyo Metro and Toei Subway lines are labeled with a colored circle and a single letter) and scan your IC Card using the card reader. Double-check which direction you're headed (do the station numbers go up or down?) and go to the appropriate platform.

- On escalators, stand to the left and walk to the right. On staircases, arrows indicate which side to take, depending on whether you're going up or down. That said, in every station there are locals who don't adhere to the rules. Whether you do is up to you!

- Once you reach the platform, form a single-file line. Markings on the floor indicate where to line up in front of each train door.

- Sometimes you'll see a pink rectangle on the floor that says, "Women Only." These indicate train cars reserved for women during rush hours, a policy introduced to reduce sexual harassment. The exact times of the women-only rule varies by company. The rule is usually in effect from 7:30 a.m. to 9:30 a.m., but it could also be valid 24 hours a day. So pay attention, men, even though there is no fine for breaking the rule.

- When the train arrives at the station, let the passengers get off, then follow the people ahead of you in line to board the train. If the train is packed, you may want to let other people on ahead of you. That way you'll be first in line to get on the next train, which will likely arrive in just a few minutes.

HELP! I FORGOT MY IC CARD!

- Go to any ticket window and tell the employee which station you want to go to.

  __________駅に行きたい: _______ eki ni kitai : _____ [eh-kee nee-kee-ty]: I want to go to ___ station

- The employee will figure out the cost of the ride, sell you the right ticket, and write down the route for you (try to get the alphanumeric code of the stations).

- You can also figure out the cost yourself using the map at the station's entrance.

- If you have to switch rail companies to transfer, you'll need to buy a ticket at the other company's ticket window.

- Once you arrive at your destination station, insert the ticket into the slot at the turnstile. It won't come back out.

ON THE **SUBWAY**

Credit: Cfktj1596

All subway seats are laid out the same way, against the sides of the car, leaving as much room in the middle as possible. If there are no seats, hold on to one of the handles provided. If the seats face forward, you're on a major line.

The six seats at the front and back of each car are for people who are elderly, disabled, or pregnant. You can sit in them if they're open, but you must give them up to priority passengers as needed.

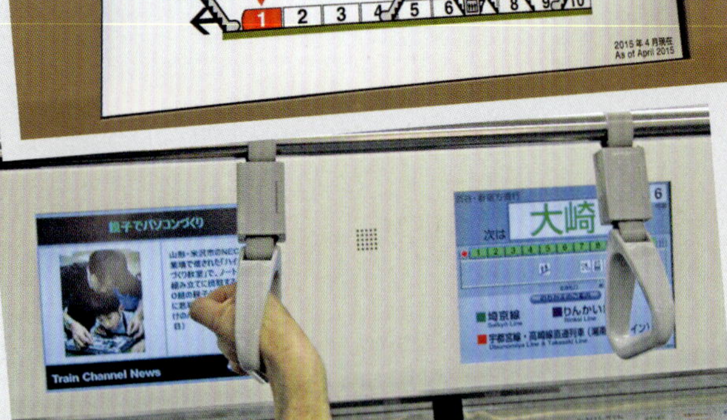

Credit: Steven Vance

Credit: mia!

If you find a place to sit and are carrying bags, you have three options:

Place them on the overhead shelf	Hold them on your lap	Place them on the floor between your feet

Be considerate of other passengers. Don't take phone calls on the subway! Do as the locals do and text instead.

Food and drinks are prohibited. However, this rule no longer applies on major lines in seats with fold-down tables.

The screens above the train doors are full of information, including:

- The time between stations.
- Transfers available at the next station.
- The location of stairs, escalators, and elevators at the next stop.
- Which doors (left or right) will open at the next stop.

Keep an ear out as well. The name of the station will be announced before each stop, as well as the available transfers—first in Japanese, then in English. Also, the chime that plays upon arrival is different for every station! Memorize the chime for the station nearest your hotel to help you remember where to get off.

TIP!

If you're pregnant, ask for a ninshin badge [neen-sheen bah-ah-jee] at one of the major JR stations, in case an inconsiderate person demands proof before letting you sit in the reserved seats.

GETTING **OFF**

LIFE HACK!

If you're stuck in the middle of the train and need to get off at the next station, yell "ORIMASU" [oh-lee-mass]! It means "I'm getting off!" and works even better if you're a foreigner. Don't be afraid to force your way through the crowd—making sure to say "Sumimasen" (pardon me), of course.

TRANSFERS

- If you're transferring to another train with the same company (Tokyo Metro/Toei Subway or JR), look up for the white signs. Find the icon for your line and follow it to the next platform.

- If you're switching companies, look for the yellow signs and follow them to the correct exit.

- Continue to the turnstiles, where you'll pay for your trip. Keep following the signs. In some stations (Ueno, Shibuya) you might even have to go outdoors to transfer between stations.

- Once you arrive at the transfer station, scan your IC Card and head for the correct platform.

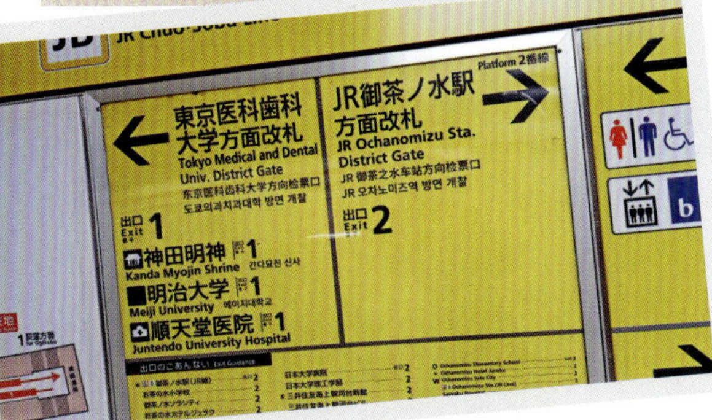

HELP! MY IC CARD RAN OUT!

It always happens at the worst times. You scan your IC Card and hear the sound and see the red light that means your card is empty. Recharge it at a machine or ticket window.

EXITING THE STATION

Once you've arrived at your destination station, it's time to resurface aboveground. But taking the wrong exit can cause significant detours at stations like Shinjuku, which has over two hundred exits!

LIFE HACK!
Duck under an escalator or staircase for a moment to wait until the platform clears out.

Look for the bright yellow signage posted next to maps. They list the top nearby landmarks and the name and number of the exit to take.

JR stations name their exits (North/East/South/West/Central).

At large stations, look for the name/number of your exit.

If you don't find what you're looking for, speak with an employee on the platform or at the nearest ticket window.

I want to go to ___. Where is the exit for ___?

___ に行きたい. ___ の出口はどこですか？

___ ni ikitai. ___ no deguchi wa doko desuka?

___ nee ee-kee-tay. ___ no day-goo-chee wah doh-koh day-ska?

Look up for the yellow signs to find your exit number. NOTE: Sometimes exits are grouped by number until you get nearer to them. For example, if you're looking for exit 7, follow the signs for exits 5–8. Once you get closer, signs will point you in different directions for exits 5, 6, 7, and 8.

Pass through the turnstiles and keep going until you exit the station.

HELP! I MISSED MY STOP!

You were daydreaming and missed your stop and now you've gone one or two stops past it. Don't panic. Get off the train at the next stop, head to the opposite platform, and take the train heading the other direction. Your IC Card won't even be charged for it. The only thing you'll have lost is a few minutes of your time.

Credit: Stephanie Ah-fa

MAJOR SUBWAY STATIONS
YAMANOTE

The six train stations listed in this section are JR's official primary stations. They are designed to be tourist-friendly and employ English-speaking staff. You can also show your voucher at these stations to pick up your JR Pass and obtain a pregnancy badge.

SHINJUKU

JR	Odakyū	Keiō Line	Toei Subway	Tokyo Metro
JY17	OH01	KO01	S01	M08
JC05			E27	
JB10				
JA11				

With 3.5 million daily passengers, Shinjuku is the world's busiest train station. It also has the most English-speaking employees available. Don't hesitate to ask for directions. Even locals get lost in the labyrinthine corridors.

Here are some shortcuts to save you time:
• JR lines are near the south and east entrances.
• Tokyo Metro/Toei Subway lines are near the west entrance (except the Marunouchi line, which is on the east side).
• The Odakyū lines are near the south entrance.
• The Keiō lines are near the west entrance.

East Exit / Central East Exit: Kabukichō district (3, 5, 7, 9, 11), Golden Gai district (15)

West Exit / Central West Exit: Tokyo Metropolitan Government Building, Omoide Yokochō district

South Exit: Shinjuku Gyoen National Garden (2 at station M10 Shinjuku-Gyoemmae)

Credit: Nesnad

IKEBUKURO

JR	Tōbu	Seibu	Tokyo Metro
JY13	TJ01	SI01	M25
JA12			Y09
			F09

The turnstiles are on the northwest side, but the station has various entrances for the various companies. Don't confuse the Seibu East Exit with the East Exit or the Seibu South Exit (on the east side) with the Tōbu Line's South Exit (on the west side).

East Exit: Sunshine City (35)

Credit: Wei-Te Wong

UENO

JR	Tokyo Metro
JY05 – JU02	G16
JJ01 – JK30	H17

Ueno is the most popular downtown station for travelers coming from Narita. The turnstiles are located on the northeast side. Be careful when making transfers. Some of the tunnels are just over five feet high!

Park Exit: Ueno Zoo and Park (7, 9)

TOKYO

JR	Tokyo Metro
JY01 – JC01	M17
JE01 – JT01	
JU01 – JK26	
JO19	
Shinkansen	

Tokyo station is the terminus for the west- and northbound Shinkansen trains. Its underground mall includes shops selling Japanese pop culture items. The redbrick building was constructed in 1914 and is a tourist attraction in its own right.

Marunouchi North Exit: Imperial Palace East Gardens (M9)

SHINAGAWA

JR	Keikyū
JY25 – JK20 – JO17 JT03 – Shinkansen	KK01

Shinagawa is the southernmost station in Yamanote and, like Ueno, a major hub for Shinkansen trains from the west, Haneda airport shuttles, and suburban trains, as its massive covered corridors suggest.

Takanawa Exit: Maxell Aqua Park Shinagawa

SHIBUYA

JR	Tōkyū	Tokyo Metro	Keiō
JY20 – JA10	DT01 – TY01	Z01 – F16 G01	IN01

Famous for its massive intersection, Shibuya underwent a decade of construction to prepare for the influx of tourists for the 2020 Olympics. It is the number one station for any and all transit information.

Hachikō Exit: Hachikō statue, Shibuya Crossing (8)

OTHER STATIONS YOU SHOULD KNOW

AKIHABARA

JR	Tokyo Metro
JY03 – JB19 – JK28	H15

The Yamanote and Chūō-Sōbu lines meet at Akihabara station, which lies at the center of the otaku district.

OCHANOMIZU

JR	Tokyo Metro
JC03 – JB18	M20

Located partway between Chūō and Chūō-Sōbu, Ochanomizu station is the major station for both lines. You can switch between local and express trains there.

NOTE!

You'll have to exit the station and go outside to transfer between the JR and Tokyo Metro lines!

ŌTEMACHI

Toei Subway	Tokyo Metro
I09	C11 – T09 M18 – Z08

Primary hub for five subway lines.

KŌRAKUEN AND KASUGA

Tokyo Metro	Toei Subway
M22 – N11	E07 – I12

IIDABASHI

JR	Toei Subway	Tokyo Metro
JB16	E06	N10 – T06 Y13

Primary hub for four subway lines, access to JR.

AKASAKA MITSUKE AND NAGATACHŌ

Tokyo Metro
G05 – M13 and N07 – Z04 – Y16

These two stations neighbor each other, so you can transfer directly from one to the other via underground tunnels.

COIN LOCKERS

Locals use coin lockers every day to store their belongings. Highly recommended!

WHERE TO FIND THEM

Most stations offer coin lockers to store luggage. Busier stations have more of them, as you would expect. Major stations use a Locker Search touchscreen in Suica's brand colors showing you where coin lockers are located. A color code indicates how many lockers are vacant.

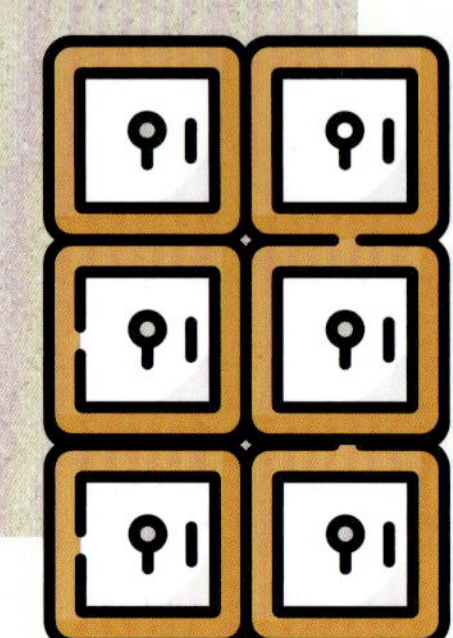

Coin Locker
コインロッカー
koinrokkā
[koh-een lo-kah-ah]

Credit: Tennen-Gas

COST

The cost depends on the station and the size of the locker.

Small
- About 12" high
- ¥300–¥400

Most common size

Medium
- About 21" high
- ¥400–¥500

Fewer available

Large
- About 33" high
- ¥600–¥800

Mostly available at major stations

There are extra-large lockers nearly five feet high, but these are exceedingly rare.

DROP OFF

- Find an empty locker in the desired size. Colored lights or latches indicate whether the locker is available (red means it's in use, green means it's vacant).

OR

- Touch the screen. Press "English," then "Checking" to see which lockers are free.

- Open the locker door, deposit your belongings, and close the door.
- Close the latch. The screen will display a message in Japanese.
- If you haven't already, press "English."
- Check that the locker number matches the number you selected and press "Confirm."
- Choose your payment method (IC Card or cash).
- Take your receipt. Don't lose it!
- LIFE HACK! Take a picture of your receipt in case you lose it.

PICK UP

Touch the screen. Select "English."

Press "Taking Out."

Enter your PIN.

Enter the numerical code on your receipt and press "Confirm."

Retrieve your belongings.

IC CARD SHORTCUT

If you paid by IC Card, select that option when picking up your bags. The computer will search for your card automatically and open the locker.

TIP!
You won't be able to use this feature if you recharged your IC Card after depositing your luggage. You'll need to enter your PIN instead, so don't throw away your receipt! It's worth the minor inconvenience to recharge your IC Card.

STORAGE TIME

Station employees clear out lockers every three days. That means you have 48 to 72 hours to fetch your belongings.

LOST **AND FOUND**

You reach for your umbrella, camera, or bag and realize it's gone. You know you had it when you got on the train. Rest assured, you're far from alone. Each year, JR and Tokyo Metro process 2.2 million and 4 million lost items, respectively! You have an excellent chance of being reunited with your item, especially if you follow these steps.

STEP 1

While your memory is fresh, note all the details you can think of regarding where you might have lost your item:

- Which subway line were you on?
- Which stations were you between?
- At what time did you lose it?
- Were you nearer the front or the back of the train?
- Did you stow the item above or below the seat?

STEP 2

Go back to the station you arrived at. Explain the situation to the staff at the ticket window. They will direct you to the nearest lost and found office. If you're lucky, your station will have one. Otherwise, you'll have to take the subway to get there.

Lost and found offices are marked on maps with this icon. Or ask a station employee for directions.

Lost item
忘れ物
wasuremono
[wah-soo-lay-mo-no]

Lost and found office
お忘れ物承り所
owasuremono no azukari-shō
[oh-wah-soo-lay-mo-no no ah-zoo-kah-ree-sho-oh]

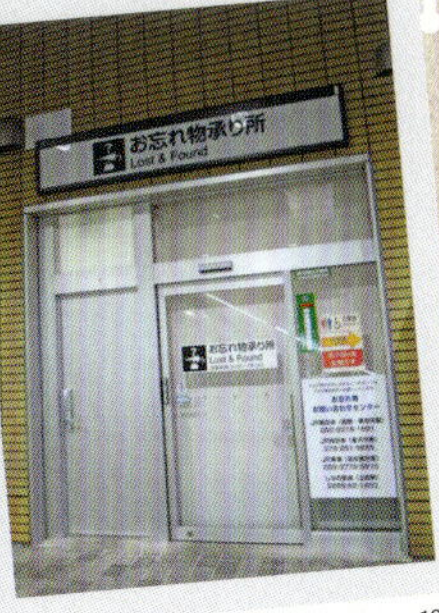

Report the lost item. Provide as many details as you can on the item itself and where you might have lost it.

Size	Brand
Color	Distinctive marking

Credit: Komakoma1998

TIP!

Label as many bags and valuables as you can with your name and email address. Include your hotel's business card so that lost and found employees can contact them. A few lucky tourists have arrived at their hotel to find their lost item waiting for them.

STEP 3

You'll discover right away whether your item has been found. If so, you can pick it up at a lost and found office. NOTE: Often the office is located at the line's terminus. In urgent cases, the railway company may give you free tickets to get there. But if you're not in a hurry, ask to pick it up the next day at the lost and found office that's most convenient for you.

If your item *hasn't* been found, you'll be given an inquiry number for the next time you call. Leave your email address and the phone number of your hotel.

Credit: 小倉商事

TAKING **THE BUS**

Unlike the trains and subway, buses frequently arrive a few minutes late. Each company operates its buses in different ways.

NOTE!

The Japanese drive on the left. That means the bus will arrive at the bus stop from the right.

TIP!

Not all buses display stops in English. Use Google Maps to figure out where you are.

TOEI BUS (WITHIN THE 23 WARDS)

- Get out your change (¥210 for adults, ¥110 for children) or IC Card.
- Board the bus through the front door.
- Pay with your change or a ¥1,000 bill (and retrieve the change) or use your IC Card.
- Choose a seat. NOTE: The seats are very small. Alternatively, you may choose to stand and hold on to one of the handles.
- Check the screen above the driver for the next stop. The driver will always announce the next stop as it gets nearer.
- If it's the stop you want, press the button marked とまります (exit) and leave via the back door.

Credit: Ryosuke Yagi

Credit: LHOON

Credit: LHOON

OTHER BUSES (OUTSKIRTS OF TOKYO)

- Board the bus through the back door and take a ticket from the dispenser.

OR

- Scan your IC Card.

- Check the number on your ticket. Find your number on the map above the driver to determine how much you owe. Get out your change.
- Choose a seat. NOTE: The seats are very small. Alternatively, you may choose to stand and hold on to one of the handles.
- Check the screen above the driver for the next stop. The driver will always announce the next stop as it gets nearer.
- Insert your ticket in the machine next to the driver and pay with your change or a ¥1,000 bill (and retrieve the change) or scan your IC Card.
- If you have a JR Pass, show it to the driver.
- Exit through the front door.

If you're not sure whether to board in the front or back, simply follow the other passengers. Or look for the signs:

Enter
入口

Exit
出口

TAXIS

WHAT THEY **LOOK LIKE**

Taxicabs differ in color depending on the company, but they are all recognizable by the light-up sign on the roof or a green license plate.

WHERE TO FIND THEM

- At taxi stands near major subway stations.
- Using the JapanTaxi app, available in English.
- Hail one on the street.

Taxi
タクシー
takushii
[tah-koo-shee-ee]

Taxi Stand
タクシー乗り場
takushii noriba
[tah-koo-shee-ee no-ree-bah]

AVAILABILITY

Daytime: A sign on the taxi's dashboard indicates whether it is available:

空車 (kūsha) means it's available, 賃走 (chinsō) means it's occupied.

The color code may seem counterintuitive:

RED means it's available, GREEN/BLUE means it's occupied.

Nighttime: Only taxis with their roof sign illuminated are available.

Vacant	Occupied
空車	賃走
kūsha	*chinsō*
RED	BLUE

- Don't try to open the door yourself. It will open and close automatically. If you are traveling with large suitcases, let the driver load them into the trunk and don't try to help. Scratching the car even the tiniest bit will cost you greatly, so don't take the risk, even if the driver looks like they could use assistance.

- Taxis can carry up to four passengers, one in the front seat and three in the back.

- Drivers rarely speak English. Make sure you have the address of your destination written down in Japanese.

- USB chargers are available for you to charge your phone during the ride. Some companies sell bottles of water (¥100) or umbrellas (¥500).

Credit: Hajime Nagahata

Taxis are extremely expensive: ¥410 for the first kilometer, increasing by ¥80 every 237 m. At night (10 p.m. to 5 a.m.), rates are 20% higher.

There are three payment methods:

- Credit card (sometimes)
- IC Card
- Cash (no tip necessary)

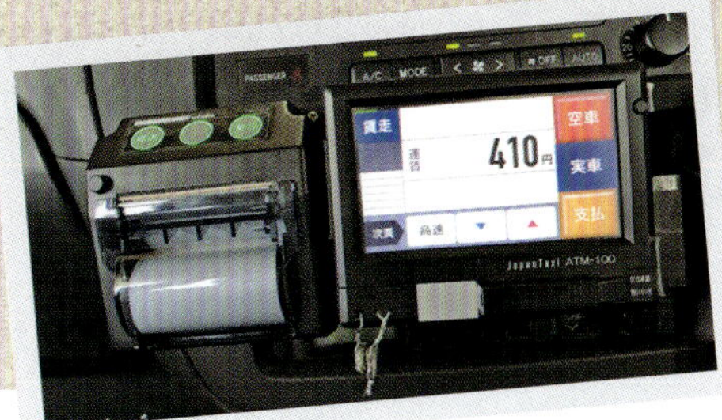

Get a receipt at the end of the ride. Hold on to it, at least for a while. It contains the taxi company's phone number in case you left something in the cab. Some companies even have a hotline available in English.

Wait for the doors to open and close automatically and let the driver unload your bags. Then you're off to your destination.

TOKYO **ON FOOT**

Watch out for cyclists, who ride on even the narrowest of sidewalks, often paying little heed to pedestrians.

NO JAYWALKING

NOTE!

Traffic lights turn green for cars at the same time that the "don't walk" signal appears for pedestrians. Wait for the "walk" signal to cross, and always cross at crosswalks.

Sometimes you'll have to stop to let a train pass by. As the train approaches, arms will automatically come down, accompanied by lights and alarms. You might have to wait two or three minutes to let multiple trains pass, so wait for the all clear!

TIP!

Look up! Tokyo is a vertical city with many shops and stores above the ground floor. But take note: Some upstairs restaurants advertise at street level. If you're not careful, you might end up eating at a different establishment than the one you wanted!

NOTE!

You might come across public maps to help you find your way. Be aware that the top of the map isn't always north. An arrow will indicate which way is north, which can vary even between maps just a hundred meters apart. Maps face the direction you're going.

KANJI YOU SHOULD KNOW

Stop

止まれ  とまれ

tomare
[toh-mah-lay]

When you see this written on the ground or on a sign, stop.

BIKESHARES

Docomo is a private company that has installed around 700 bikeshare stations. To rent a bike, you must register on the company's website, available in English:
https://docomo-cycle.jp/tokyo-project/en_index.html

Information is available in English, along with a video explaining how the stations work.

NOTE!

The Japanese drive—and ride—on the left!

NOTE!

Be careful where you park your bike. Parking in a prohibited area may result in a fine. Or worse, the bike may even be impounded! The police are serious about bike parking. Look around to make sure there are no signs prohibiting you from parking your bike there.

Credit: SLTc

JAPANESE **ADDRESSES**

You know you're in the vicinity of your destination and you have the street address. But finding the location may not be as simple as you think.

Japanese addresses provide increasingly specific details to locate buildings:

Prefecture	City	District	Block	Building number
都道府県	市	丁目	番地	号
todōfuken	shi	chōme	banchi	gō

For example, if you're looking for the tourism office in Asakusa district, the address is:
2 chme-18-9 Kaminarimon, Taitō-ku, Tokyo 111-0034, Japan

111-0034	Tokyo	Taitō-ku	Kaminarimon	2-18-9
postal code	**city**	**ward**	**district**	**building 9 on block 18 in section 2 of the district**

NOTE!

Buildings are numbered chronologically. The first building to be constructed is number 1, followed by number 2—but they might not be next to each other! To complicate matters, if building 1 is demolished to make way for a new building, the new structure will receive a new number— and there will never be a building 1 on the block again!

As you may have noticed, street names mean nothing. Many addresses don't even have them!

You can find street names on metal signs on street corners, usually on a pole or affixed to a wall.

Most Japanese addresses are accompanied by a map to help you find them. Don't hesitate to ask for a map rather than an address.

Credit: Comyu

If, despite your best efforts and even Google Maps, you can't find your destination, there are two establishments that might help.

Post office

If you spot the logo for the Japanese post office (see p. 20), head inside. Mail carriers know the area like the back of their hands and can help you out.

Kōban (see p. 65)

Every district has a police booth with agents available 24 hours a day to help find lost items, handle neighborhood grievances . . . and orient lost tourists. With a little luck, one of the agents can help you to your destination.

NOTE!

Even taxi drivers can get confused by local addresses. If you take a taxi back to your hotel, keep an eye out once you get close so you can guide the driver to the hotel if necessary.

Credit: Lombroso

Credit: Eric

Credit: Kentin

TAKING THE **SHINKANSEN**

There's more to Japan than just Tokyo. Maybe you've made plans to venture outside the capital and explore the rest of the country. If so, the best form of transport is Japan's world-famous bullet train, the Shinkansen!

WHERE TO GO

West

There are three types of Shinkansen that run along the Tokyo–Osaka line:

NOZOMI: The fastest, but serves only five stations: Shinagawa, Shin-Yokohama, Nagoya, Kyoto, and Osaka.

HIKARI: Serves more stations.

KODAMA: The slowest. A local train that gets you to Osaka in about four hours.

NOTE!
There are only two places in Tokyo to catch these trains: Tokyo and Shinagawa stations.

North

There are three types of Shinkansen that run along the Tokyo–Shin–Hakodate line:

HAYABUSA: Not only the fastest train but the only one that goes to the Shin-Hakodate terminus.

YAMABIKO: A slower train that terminates at Morioka.

NASUNO: The shortest line, terminating at Kōriyama station.

NOTE!
There are only two places in Tokyo to catch these trains: Tokyo and Ueno stations.

Shinkansen fares are the same every single day of the year, but tickets sell out faster during certain seasons. The busiest periods are late March, early May, and early August. It's best to purchase your tickets at least 48 hours in advance for the best selection of departure times.

Where to buy tickets

You can purchase tickets at ticket windows at major JR stations (see p. 26). You can also buy them from a machine, but machines don't accept JR Passes and only take cash.

TIP!
If possible, depart from one of the three Shinkansen stations: Shinagawa (westbound), Ueno (northbound), or Tokyo (terminus for both lines). These stations have special ticket windows for tourists with employees who speak a little English.

TIP!
If traveling west, ask for a seat on the right side of the car. You'll be able to see Mount Fuji through the window!

Credit: BradBeattie

Credit: pelican

TAKING THE **SHINKANSEN**

At your departure station (Tokyo, Shinagawa, or Ueno), head for the Shinkansen platform.

- Insert your ticket into the turnstile.
- Check the signs to determine which platform your train is leaving from.
- If you have assigned seats, wait in front of the doors for your train car.
- If you don't have assigned seats, find the car for unassigned seating

TIP!
The second car usually has the most open seats.

BUYING A **TICKET**

Ticket types

Unassigned seating (Jiyūseki):
Unassigned seats are the cheapest. Seats are located at the front and back of the train. But be warned: They're first come, first served. On busy trains, you may be forced to stand up for the whole trip.

Assigned seating (Shiteiseki):
For an extra ¥2,000 or so, you can reserve an assigned seat. This is the best way to ensure you'll have a seat for the trip and, if traveling with others, that you can sit together.

First class/Green car:
All first-class seats are assigned.

NOTE!
If the dimensions of your luggage add up to more than 160 cm, you must reserve seats in the front or back of the car, the only places where you can store your luggage during the trip.

TIP!
Consider using a takkyūbin luggage delivery service (see p. 20)!

JR Pass

If you have a JR Pass, you can reserve assigned seats at no extra cost. Show your pass to the booking agent before telling them where you want to go. You'll get tickets for free!

NOTE!
If you're traveling to western Japan, the JR Pass is only valid on Hikari and Kodama trains. If you want to take a Nozomi train, you'll have to pay full price.

TIP!
If buying same-day tickets, watch the screens above the ticket window while waiting in line. Symbols indicate how full the next trains are:

○	△	✕
Lots of seats remaining	Some seats remaining	Train is full

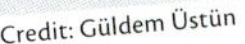

Credit: Güldem Üstün

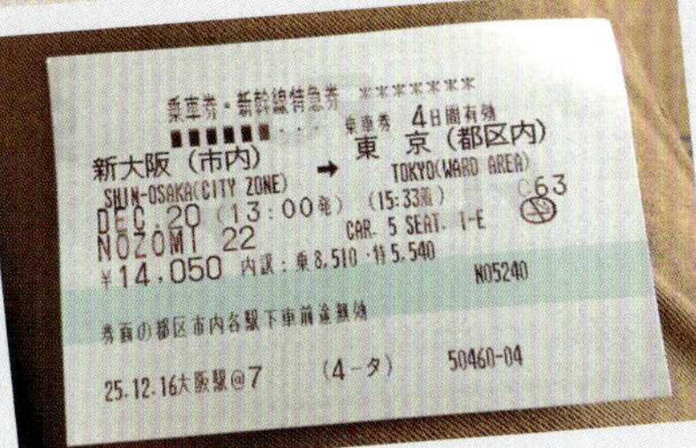

TIP!
There isn't much room for baggage—only a shelf about 16 inches high running along the length of the car. You can store your luggage at the front or back of the car, provided space is available.

TIP!
A pedal on the aisle side lets you swivel seat rows 180° so you can face each other, a handy feature when traveling in groups or with family. Plus, then you can place your bags between seat backs between rows.

ACCESSIBILITY

FOR BLIND AND VISUALLY IMPAIRED PERSONS

- Textured lines on the ground serve as a guide for people with visual impairments. However, they have a tendency to trip up rolling suitcases.

- Ask for help at the ticket window. An employee will walk you to your platform.

- Most major malls and supermarkets also offer this service. An employee will literally take you by the hand and answer any question you may have, although only in Japanese.

NOTE!
Japanese braille is different from English.

Every train platform has at least one escalator and one elevator.

Escalator
エスカレーター
esukarētā
[ess-oo-kah-lay-tah-ah]

Elevator
エレベーター
erebētā
[ell-ay-bay-tah-ah]

A map on each platform displays the position of the train cars relative to the stairs, escalators, and elevators, allowing you to plan your route. Train cars also display a map of the next station on a screen as the train pulls in.

TIP!
Major crosswalks feature audible signals that tell you when to cross. Usually, the signal is a bird chirp (frequently the iconic cuckoo call). At major intersections (Shibuya, Shinjuku, Ueno, Ikebukuro) the sound plays automatically, but in other places you have to press a button to activate it.

NOTE!
All buildings have elevators. They even appear in the unlikeliest of places, such as the ancient Sensō-ji temple in Asakusa.

Credit: Lombroso

FOR PERSONS WITH **LIMITED MOBILITY**

- If you use a wheelchair, go to the subway ticket window. An employee will help you get to your platform via a ramp that leads directly to a wheelchair-accessible train car. They will then notify an employee at your destination station, who will be waiting for you right outside your car to help you transfer or exit the station.

- Underground stations have at least one wheelchair-friendly way to get downstairs—although it can require quite the detour. It will either be an elevator or a gentle ramp.

- Most Japanese escalators have a wheelchair feature in which three steps remain flat to create a platform for your wheelchair with a safety guardrail. Only an employee can activate the feature, so you'll have to ask for help.

- Bus drivers will get off to help you board using a folding ramp. They'll ask for your destination so they can help you get off.

- Taxi drivers will help you climb into the back seat and then load your chair into the trunk. If you have an electric wheelchair, you'll need to book a van equipped for your needs in advance. You can also ask a taxi driver at any train station. They'll radio in to order you a suitable taxi as soon as possible.

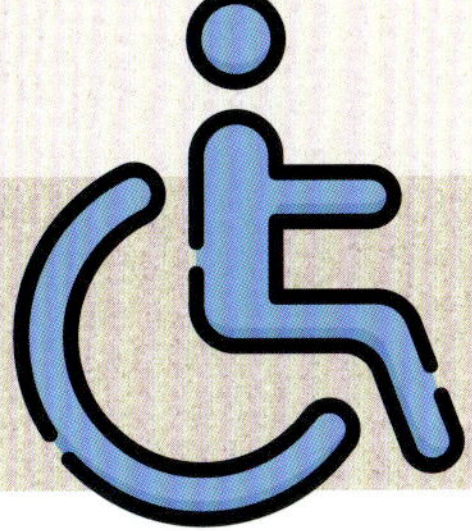

www.accessible-japan.com

Credit: DAIF

KEY WORDS AND PHRASES

Post office
郵便局
yuubinkyoku
[yoo-oo-been-kee-oh-koo]

Coin locker
コインロッカー
koinrokkā
[koh-een lo-kah-ah]

Luggage delivery
宅急便
takkyūbin
[tah-kee-oo-oo-been]

Station employee
駅員
ekiin
[ay-kee-een]

I want to go to ___ station
…駅に行きたい.
... eki ni kitai.
[___ ay-kee nee ee-kee-ty]

I want to go to ___.
… に行きたい.
... ni ikitai.
[___ nee ee-kee-ty]

Where is the exit for ___?
… の出口はどこですか?
... no deguchi wa doko desuka ?
[___ noh day-goo-chee wah doh-koh day-ska]

Credit: JKT-c

Station
駅
eki
[ay-kee]

Train
電車
densha
[den-shah]

Bus
バス
basu
[bah-soo]

Bus stop
バス停
basutei
[bah-soo-tay]

Taxi
タクシー
takushii
[tah-koo-shee-ee]

Taxi stand
タクシー乗り場
takushii noriba
[tah-koo-shee-ee noh-ree-bah]

Post office
郵便局
yuubinkyoku
[yoo-oo-been-kee-oh-koo]

Restroom
トイレ
toire
[toh-ee-lay]

Police station
交番
kōban
[koh-oh-bahn]

Airport
空港
kuukou
[koo-oo-koh-oh]

Boat
舟
fune
[foo-nay]

Ticket window
窓口
mado guchi
[mah-doh goo-chee]

One-way trip
片道
kata michi
[kah-tah mee-chee]

Round trip
往復
ou fuku
[oh-oh foo-koo]

Assigned seat
指定席
shitei seki
[shee-tay say-kee]

Unassigned seat
自由席
jiyuu seki
[jee-yoo-oo say-kee]

Window seat
窓側の席
mado gawa no seki
[mah-doh gah-wah no say-kee]

Aisle seat
通路側の席
tsūro gawa no seki
[tsoo-lo gah-wah no say-kee]

Seat number
座席番号
zaseki bangō
[zah-say-kee bahn-go-oh]

I lost ___.
…をなくしてしまいました。
... wo nakushite shimaimashita.
[___ oh nah-koo-shee-tay shee-my-mah-shee-tah]

Credit: Rsa

Entrance
入り口
iriguchi
[ee-ree-goo-chee]

Exit
出口
deguchi
[day-goo-chee]

Map
地図
chizu
[chee-zoo]

Is there a map?
地図はありますか?
Chizu wa arimasuka ?
[chee-zoo wah ah-lee-mah-soo-kah]

Above
上
ue
[oo-ay]

Below
下
shita
[shee-tah]

Inside
中
naka
[nah-kah]

In front
前
mae
[mah-ay]

Behind
後ろ
ushiro
[oo-shee-ro]

Next to
…の隣
... no tonari
[___ no toh-nah-lee]

Near
近く
chikaku
[chee-kah-koo]

Across
向かい側
mukaigawa
[moo-ky-gah-wah]

Floor
階
kai
[ky]

Stairs
階段
kaidan
[ky-dahn]

QUESTIONS

Where am I?

ここはどこ？

Koko wa doko ?

[koh-koh wah doh-koh]

Where is the station?

駅はどこ
ですか？

Eki wa doko desuka ?

[ay-kee wah doh-koh
day-ska]

Where is the platform for ___?

...行きの乗り場は
どこですか？

... iki no noriba wa doko
desuka ?

[___ ee-kee no no-lee-bah
wah doh-koh day-ska]

What time is the next bus?

次のバスは何時
ですか？

Tsugi no basu wa nan-ji
desu ka ?

[tsoo-ghee no bah-soo wah
nahn-jee day-ska]

What time does the next train leave?

終電は何時
ですか。

Shūden wa nan-ji desu ka ?

[shoo-oo-den wah nahn-jee
day-ska]

When does the train leave?

電車はいつ出発
しますか？

Densha wa itsu
shuppatsu shimasu ka?

[den-shah wah ee-tsoo
shoo-Ø-pah-tsoo shee-
mah-ska]

Does this train stop at ___?

この電車は...で止
まりますか？

Kono densha wa ... de
tomarimasuka ?

[koh-no den-shah wah ___
day toh-mah-ree-mah-ska]

Where do I transfer to get to ___?

どこで...行きに乗
り換えますか？

Doko de ... iki ni
norikaemasu ka ?

[doh-koh ___ ee-kee no-
lee-kah-ay-mah-ska]

Where does this bus go?

このバスはどこ
に行きますか？

Kono basu wa doko ni
ikimasuka ?

[koh-noh bah-soo wah
doh-koh nee ee-kee-mah-
ska]

How do I get to ___?

...までどうやってい
きますか？

... made dōyatte
ikimasuka ?

[___ mah-day doh-oh-yah-Ø-
tay ee-kee-mah-ska]

ANSWERS

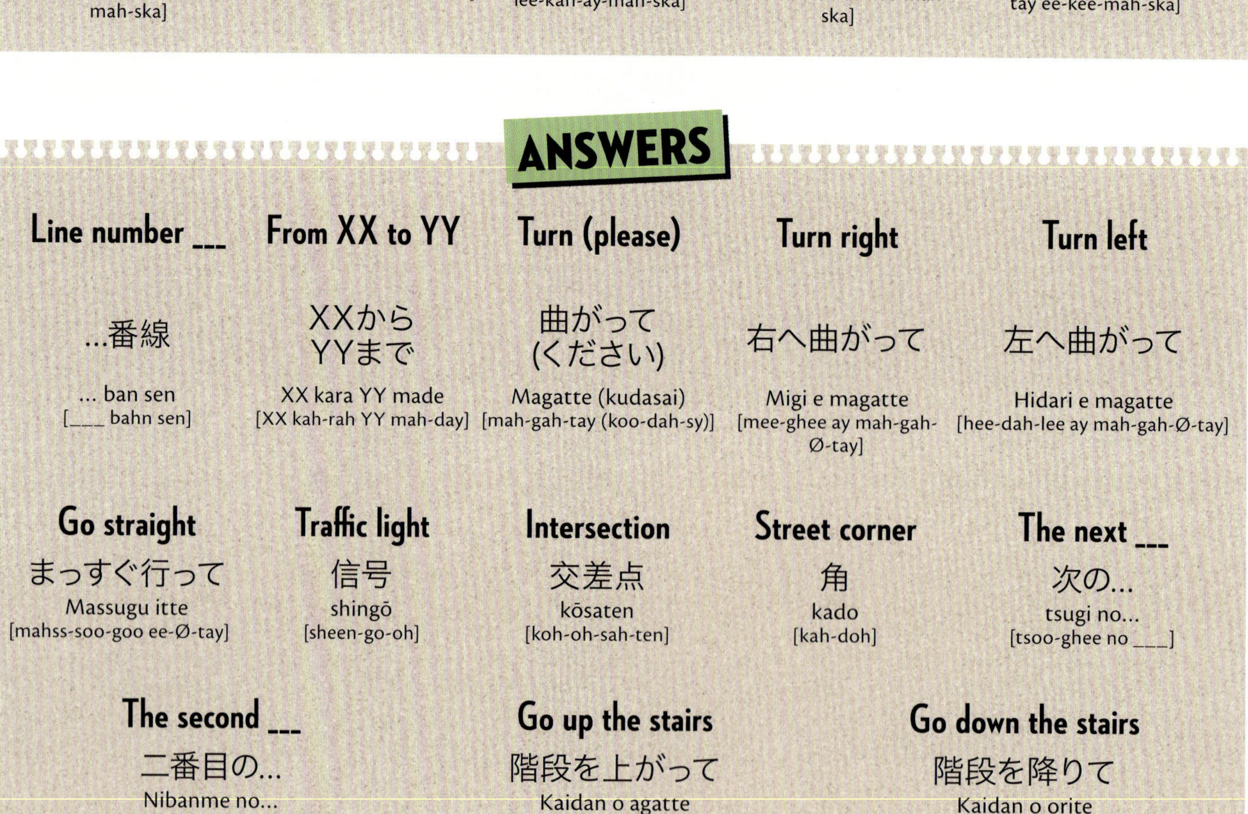

Line number ___

...番線

... ban sen
[___ bahn sen]

From XX to YY

XXから
YYまで

XX kara YY made
[XX kah-rah YY mah-day]

Turn (please)

曲がって
（ください）

Magatte (kudasai)
[mah-gah-tay (koo-dah-sy)]

Turn right

右へ曲がって

Migi e magatte
[mee-ghee ay mah-gah-
Ø-tay]

Turn left

左へ曲がって

Hidari e magatte
[hee-dah-lee ay mah-gah-Ø-tay]

Go straight

まっすぐ行って

Massugu itte
[mahss-soo-goo ee-Ø-tay]

Traffic light

信号

shingō
[sheen-go-oh]

Intersection

交差点

kōsaten
[koh-oh-sah-ten]

Street corner

角

kado
[kah-doh]

The next ___

次の...

tsugi no...
[tsoo-ghee no ___]

The second ___

二番目の...

Nibanme no...
[nee-bahn-may no ___]

Go up the stairs

階段を上がって

Kaidan o agatte
[ky-dahn oh ah-gah-Ø-tay]

Go down the stairs

階段を降りて

Kaidan o orite
[ky-dahn oh oh-lee-tay]

DAY-TO-DAY

THE YEN 円

You'll be reaching for your wallet daily, so you might as well get to know Japanese currency.

PRONUNCIATION

NOTE!

"Yen" is pronounced [en], without the Y. It sounds just like the letter N.

You'll see prices written three different ways: using the Japanese character, the international currency symbol, or in English letters.

Twelve hundred yen could be written as:

1,200 円 / ¥1,200 / 1,200 YEN

Thousands (and millions) are separated by commas, just like in America.

The exchange rate between the yen and dollar can fluctuate significantly:

$1 = 100 円 (low end)

and $1 = 160 円 (high end)

It has been hovering mostly around $1 = 140 円 in recent years.

円	$
10	0.07
100	0.71
1 000	7
1 250	9
2 000	14
2 500	18
3 000	21
4 000	29
5 000	36
10 000	71

WITHDRAWING CASH

Most ATMs don't accept international cards, or they charge extra fees for international transactions. The three reliable, no-cost ways to withdraw cash are at:

Post offices: ATMs are not available for use when offices are closed.

Prestia banks: ATMs are not available for use when offices are closed.

7-11 konbini: ATMs are available 24 hours a day.

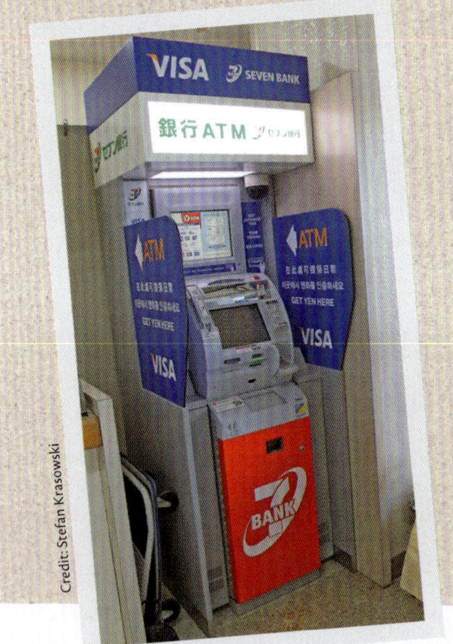

Credit: Stefan Krasowski

Coin

硬貨

kōka

[koh-oh-kah]

COINS

¥1: Made of aluminum. Costs more to make than it's worth.

¥5: Has a hole in the center. The only coin without its value written in digits on it.

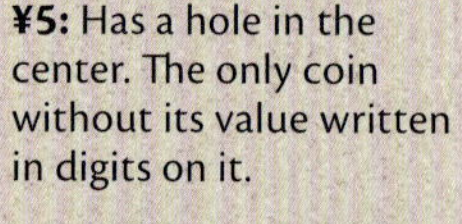

¥10: Made of copper.

¥50: Also has a hole in the center. Distinguishable from the ¥5 piece by its gray color.

¥100: The most frequently used coin, roughly equivalent to a dollar.

¥500: Easy to recognize as the largest coin of the bunch.

NOTE!

Carry a good supply of ¥100 coins. Most machines (coin lockers, vending machines, toy machines, arcade games, etc.) only accept ¥100 coins.

SALES **TAX**

Prices are always shown with and without sales tax. As of November 2025, the general sales tax rate was 10%.

The same price can be written three different ways:

1,100 円 (1,000 円 before tax)

1,100 円 (100 円 tax)

1,000 円 (1,100 円 with tax)

No matter how it's written, look at the highest number. That's the amount you'll pay.

NOTE!

Some malls have a single checkout area for all stores. Select all your items and then head to the registers.

HOW TO **PAY**

At the register, you'll see a small plastic tray for you to place your money on. Hand it to the cashier with both hands. They will recount your money, then place your change on the tray and hand it back to you. Take the tray with both hands.

More and more stores are starting to accept credit cards, but most small shops and restaurants only take cash.

TAX **EXEMPTIONS**

Many major stores waive sales tax for purchases over 5,000 円 if you show your passport. These stores display a Japan Tax Free logo.

You'll follow one of these procedures, depending on the store:

- Go to a special register, where sales tax will be subtracted BEFORE you check out.
- After you've paid, take your receipt to a special counter, where the sales tax will be refunded to you.

Change

お釣り

otsuri

[oh-tsoo-ree]

BILLS

¥1,000: The most common bill.

¥2,000: If you come across one of these, keep it! Locals don't like to use them, preferring to count in multiples of 1,000. These bills represent only 1% of bills in circulation.

¥5,000: Approximately the equivalent of a fifty-dollar bill.

¥10,000: The largest bill made. Try not to use it to pay for amounts under ¥1,000.

TIP!

Try to keep some ¥1,000 notes on hand. They're as handy as ¥100 coins.

NOTE!

In Japan, people treat their cash carefully and do their best not to crumple bills. At most, they might fold them in half. Invest in an extra-long wallet (available at any 100-yen shop) to avoid the shame of paying with wrinkled bills!

Bank note

紙幣

shihei

[shee-hay]

ETIQUETTE

Japanese etiquette can be summed up in four words: punctuality, modesty, cleanliness, and politeness.

PUNCTUALITY

People in Japan are generally on time. Being late is often considered flat-out rude.

Do your best to always arrive early to avoid disapproving looks for holding up the group, as well as long lines for public events.

NOTE!

Punctuality is particularly important for timed events, from fireworks to cherry blossom viewings. You might want to get there several hours early to grab a spot.

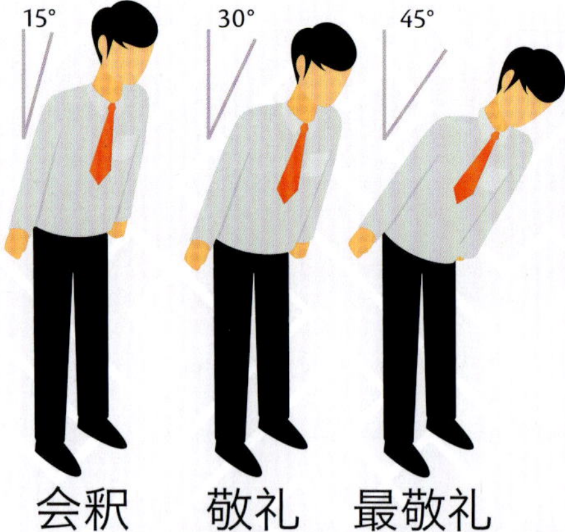

会釈
eshaku

敬礼
keirei

最敬礼
saikeirei

MODESTY

Japanese behavior is centered around humility. Japanese people try not to be noticed and will do everything they can to avoid inconveniencing others.

NOTE!

Locals will rarely say no, even if you're asking the impossible. If someone tells you "muzukashii" [moo-zoo-kah-shee-ee], meaning "it's complicated," take that as a no.

Body language can tell you a lot (see below). If the other person scratches their head, they probably mean no.

TIP!

If you give someone an expensive gift, act like it's just a cheap trinket.

NOTE!

Some Japanese people might avoid you out of fear of not being able to understand you and respond appropriately.

Avoid physical contact as much as possible. The Japanese prefer to bow.

How to bow

There are several ways to bow, depending on the circumstance.

- In most cases, an exaggerated nod, about 5°, is sufficient. Use this when you meet someone's gaze, called a mokurei [moh-koo-ray]. And smile!
- A standard bow, called an eshaku (会釈), inclines about 15°. Men keep their arms by their sides, while women clasp their hands.
- In special settings (tea ceremonies, for example), you'll perform a respectful bow or keirei (敬礼), inclining about 30°.
- For the sake of completeness, also include the extra respectful bow, the saikeirei (最敬礼), inclining about 45°.

Honorifics

- Honorifics are added to the end of a person's name to indicate varying degrees of politeness.
- San [sahn] means Mr. or Ms. This is what you should use when speaking to someone.

NOTE!

Don't use honorifics for yourself.

You'll hear other suffixes as well, including -sama, which means king or even god. It's sometimes used at restaurants when speaking to customers!

Credit: Maya-Anaïs Yataghène

CLEANLINESS

In addition to meticulous personal hygiene (see p. 62), Japanese people also keep their surroundings clean. You'll never see a local person littering, and the subway is so clean you could just about eat off the floors. And to keep their homes spotless, Japanese people remove their shoes before entering.

When to take off your shoes

- When entering an indoor space (hotel room, restaurant, etc.), check to see if the floor is raised a few inches higher than the entryway. If so, you're standing in a genkan [gen-kahn] 玄関, a traditional entryway where you should take off your shoes.

- Take off your shoes in the genkan. They shouldn't touch the raised floor. Step directly from your shoes onto the raised floor. Don slippers if available. Slippers should never be in the genkan.

- Place your shoes neatly to the side next to each other in the genkan. The heels should touch the step and the toes should face the door, the direction you'll be leaving.

- When leaving, slip into your shoes. Again, shoes should always stay in the genkan.

NOTE!

Bathrooms are considered a separate space and have their own special slippers (see p. 52).

Credit: Photocopy

Credit: m-louis.*

POLITENESS

Please

- Onegaishimasu [oh-nay-gah-ee-shee-mahss] means "please" and can be used alone in response to a question. For example, "Yes, please" = "onegaishimasu."

- A more formal way to say please is to add kudasai [koo-dah-sy] after your request. You'll hear it a lot at restaurants, on the subway, and in stores.

Thank you

There are several levels of intensity:

- Arigatō [ah-lee-gah-toh]: Thanks

- Arigatō gozaimasu [ah-lee-gah-toh goh-zay-ee-mahss]: Thank you

- Dōmo arigatō gozaimasu [doh-moh ah-lee-gah-toh goh-zay-ee-mahss]: Thank you very much

Excuse me

- Sumimasen [soo-mee-mah-sen] means "pardon me" or "coming through." It's probably the most used word in all of Japan. Just like in English, you can also use it to get someone's attention.

- To apologize for an error, use gomen nasai [goh-men nah-sy], which means something closer to "I apologize."

Hello

- Before 11 a.m., use ohayō gozaimasu [oh-hah-yoh-oh goh-zah-ee-mahss], which means "good morning."

- Between 11 a.m. and 6 p.m., use konnichiwa [koh-nee-chee-wah], which means "good day."

- After 6 p.m., use konbanwa [kon-bah-wah], or "good evening."

Presenting and recieving items

Japanese etiquette is expressed in myriad ways, even in minor interactions. If you hand someone something, use both hands, and use both hands to receive objects as well, no matter how inconsequential.

Credit: Toru Hanai, Reuters Photo

TIP!

Japanese people have a custom called omiyage [oh-mee-yah-gay] お土産, bringing home souvenirs for friends and colleagues after a trip. Keep an eye out for stores with this word on the window to find gifts to bring home.

JAPANESE **GESTURES**

Japanese people tend to be reserved and rarely express their feelings aloud. To compensate, they have developed a whole language based on gestures.

PARDON ME (COMING THROUGH)

Place your arm and hand in a sort of one-handed prayer position. Your hand should be at chest-level with your thumb facing you. Throw in a "Sumimasen!" to maneuver your way through crowds.

I'M SORRY

Place both hands in prayer position and bow.

I'M HUNGRY. LET'S EAT!

Cup your left hand at chest level, as if holding a bowl. Scoop your right index and middle fingers toward your mouth like chopsticks.

I'M THIRSTY, LET'S DRINK

Pretend to drink from a glass. This can also mean "I drank too much."

NO, YOU'RE WRONG

Wave your hand back and forth in front of your face, like a windshield wiper.

NO

When confronted with an incorrect action (such as getting confused between the entrance and exit), Japanese people cross their arms in front of themselves. They might also add, "Dame!" [dah-may], literally "not allowed."

By extension, this gesture also indicates a categorical refusal.

POINTING TO PLACES OR PEOPLE

Don't point with your finger. Use your whole hand.

POINTING TO YOURSELF

Point your index finger at your nose.

COME HERE

Wave the person over with your palm facing down.

EMBARASSMENT

Scratch the back of your head and grimace. This is often an indirect way of saying no.

OK

Form a circle with your thumb and index finger and keep the other fingers straight. You can also use a thumbs up.

I UNDERSTAND

If someone repeats themselves several times and you finally grasp what they're saying, tap your fist into the palm of the other hand to indicate that you understand.

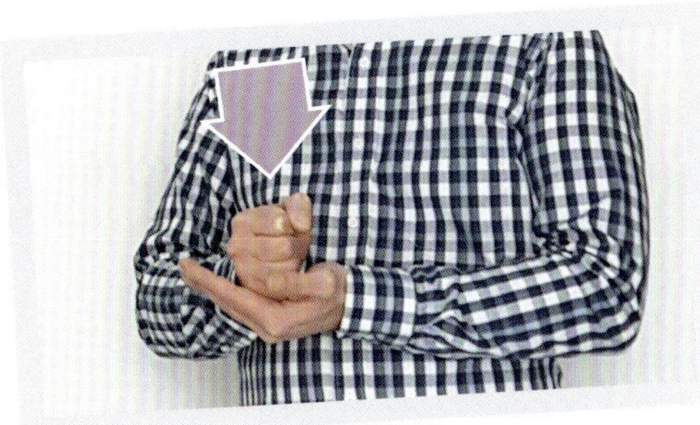

BATHROOMS

A restroom might be your first introduction to Japanese culture when you get off the plane. Here's a guide to using high-tech Japanese toilets.

Credit: Robert Basic

BIDETS

Popularized by the TOTO company, a leading manufacturer, bidets are electric toilet seats that clean your backside with a spray of water, as well as performing a number of other functions.

NOTE!

You must sit on the toilet to activate the bidet.

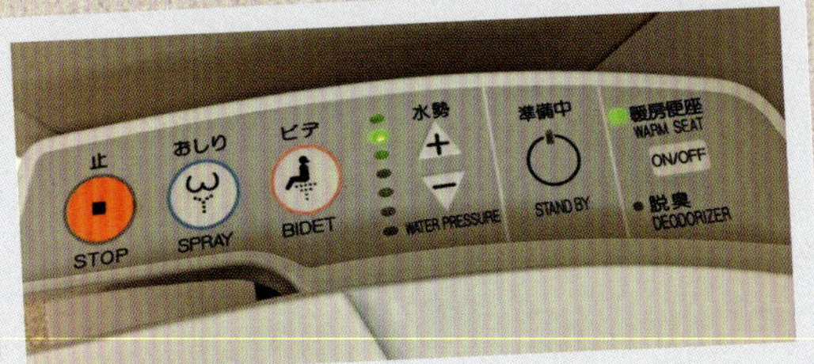

Credit: Olivier Bruchez

Controls are attached to the toilet seat or on the wall and offer a variety of features.

Buttocks	**Bidet** (for women only)	**Blow dry**	**Stop**
おしり	ビデ	乾燥	止
oshiri [oh-shee-lee]	bidet [bee-day]	kansō [kahn-soh-oh]	tome [toh-may]

OPTIONS

Water Pressure	**Weak**	**Strong**	**Water temperature**
水勢	弱	強	温水
Heated seat	**Low**	**High**	**Deodorizer**
便座	低	高	パワー脱臭

There may also be a button to play sounds of running water to mask embarrassing noises. This may be a separate device with its own switch. It's not available in all restrooms, so some women carry a portable device in their purse.

Princess sounds

音姫

otohime
[oh-toh-hee-may]

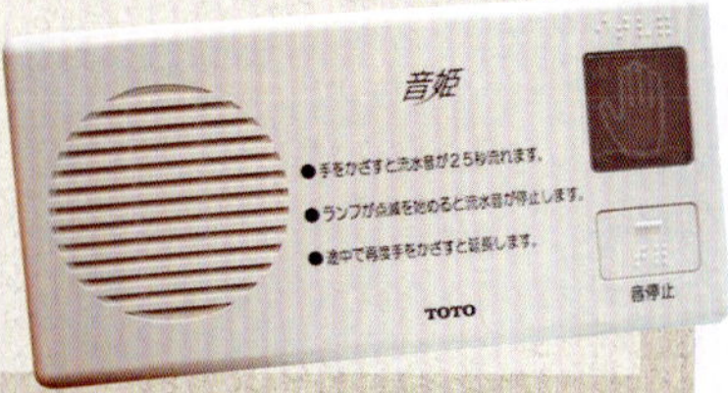

TIP!

If you only go number one, use the half flush!

Flush	**Half flush**	**Full flush**
流す	小	大

SLIPPERS

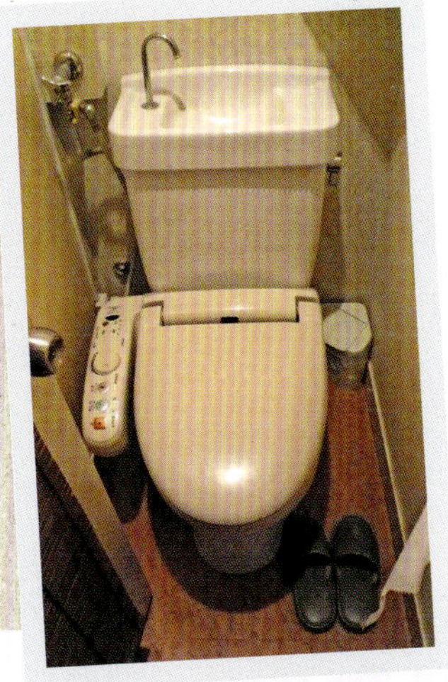

You'll frequently see slippers just inside the bathroom door. Put them on while in the bathroom and then take them off and put them back, facing away from the door, for the next person when you leave.

Credit: Cory Doctorow

WASHIKI

Washiki [wah-shee-kee] are Turkish toilets, also known as squatty potties in English. Tokyo attempted to get rid of them before the Olympics, but there's still a chance you'll run into one. Squat facing the rounded part to do your business.

Credit: Chris 73

WHERE'S THE **BATHROOM?**

If you need the restroom at a restaurant or mall, look for these characters.

Bathroom

トイレ

toire
[toh-ee-lay]

Restroom
(more polite)

お手洗い

otearai
[oh-tay-ah-lye]

How to ask where the restrooms are:

トイレはどこですか？

Toire wa doko desuka ?
[toh-ee-lay wah doh-koh day-ska]

(more polite)

お手洗いはどこですか？

Otearai wa doko desuka ?
[oh-tay-ah-lye wah doh-koh day-ska]

TIP!

If you're traveling with young children, major subway stations have areas with baby-changing tables. You'll also find them in malls, along with several other services.

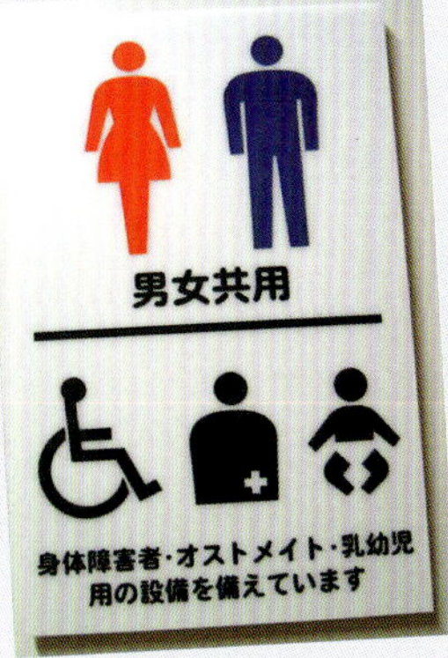

FOR **MEN**

Public urinals have a small shelf above them where you can place belongings.

Hooks are provided next to the urinals to hang your umbrella.

FAUX PAS

Certain Japanese conventions can take Westerners by surprise, but when in Tokyo, do as the Tokyoites do. Here's a glimpse of the easiest missteps to avoid, once you know about them.

BLOWING YOUR NOSE IN PUBLIC

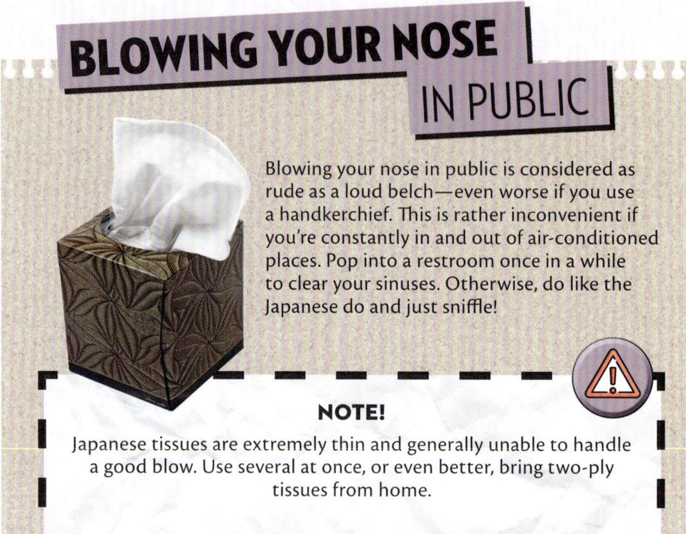

Blowing your nose in public is considered as rude as a loud belch—even worse if you use a handkerchief. This is rather inconvenient if you're constantly in and out of air-conditioned places. Pop into a restroom once in a while to clear your sinuses. Otherwise, do like the Japanese do and just sniffle!

NOTE!

Japanese tissues are extremely thin and generally unable to handle a good blow. Use several at once, or even better, bring two-ply tissues from home.

WEARING HOLEY SOCKS

If you remove your shoes upon entering a traditional establishment and your socks have holes, you'll never live down the shame. The same applies to tights and pantyhose.

COUNTING YOUR CHANGE

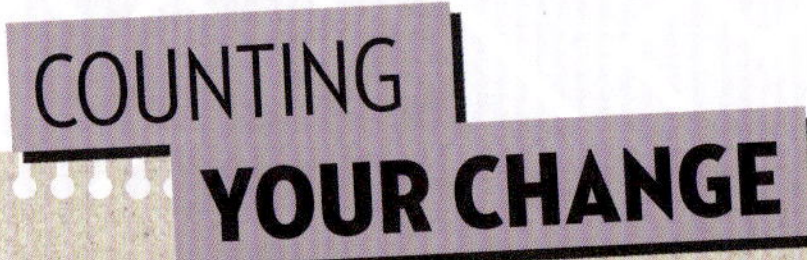

When you pay at the register, the employee will verify your change before handing it to you. Don't recount it. Doing so implies the cashier is bad at their job.

INTERRUPTING

Wait until others are done talking before you speak. This is a highly important piece of Japanese etiquette. It also stems from Japanese grammar, where the verbs and negations come at the end of the sentence.

BLOCKING THE ESCALATOR

On escalators, stand to the left single file. Leave the right side free for people to walk.

TOUCHING

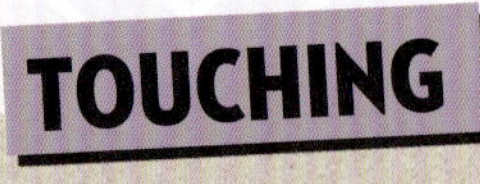

Avoid touching people, especially strangers, as much as possible. One exception is when drinking (perhaps at an izakaya; see p. 80), where you might casually pat a shoulder or leg, but no more.

TAKING **PHOTOS**

The Japanese take the use of their images very seriously. Always ask permission before photographing someone. If you want to take pictures inside a store, ask an employee.

Pardon me, may I take photos?

すみません, 写真を撮ってもいいですか？

Sumimasen, sashin wo tottemo ii desuka?
[soo-mee-mah-sen sha-sheen oh toh-Ø-tay-moh ee-ee day-ska]

Pardon me, may I photograph you?

すみません、あなたの写真を撮ってもいいですか？

Sumimasen, anata no sashin wo tottemo ii desuka?
[soo-mee-mah-sen ah-nah-tah noh sha-sheen oh toh-Ø-tay-moh ee-ee day-ska]

TIP!
Japanese smartphones are required to play a shutter sound. If you turn off the sound in your camera's settings, you can take photos quietly and discreetly.

EATING, DRINKING, OR SMOKING **WHILE WALKING**

The streets of Tokyo can be packed, and no one wants to get sauce stains or cigarette burns on their new coat. Find a bench to enjoy your snack, and only smoke in designated places or risk a fine (see p. 61).

Credit: James Abbott

MAKING NOISE ON PUBLIC TRANSPORT

Keep your conversations quiet on subways and buses. It's fine to speak at a regular volume as long as you're not disturbing your neighbors.

Credit: Antti T. Nissinen

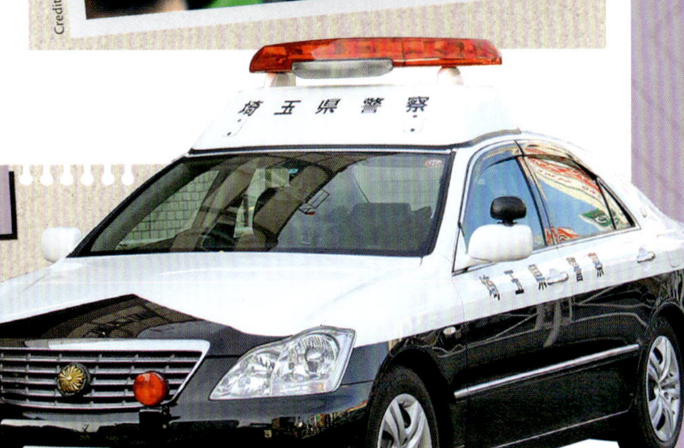
Credit: Life of Wu

REFUSING TO COOPERATE WITH **THE POLICE**

You may be stopped by the police at any time, so always carry your passport with you. Police might ask to search you even without legal authorization. Refusing to cooperate will prolong the incident.

Credit: PRiMENON

ESTABLISHMENTS

As with buses and trains, there are unwritten rules of conduct for public establishments.

BUILDINGS AND MALLS

NOTE!

Like in the USA, the ground floor is considered the first floor (1F). Basements are designated by the letter B.

Credit: RachelH_

In case of rain

Plastic bags are provided in entryways for wet umbrellas to prevent them from dripping on the floor. Insert your umbrella into the dispenser's opening and gently tug the umbrella toward you. It will come away wrapped in a plastic bag, which you can throw away when you leave.

Smaller shops also offer umbrella caddies where you can leave your umbrella in a numbered slot to prevent mix-ups and sometimes even a lock to prevent theft.

Credit: AHLN

Elevator

In an elevator, the person nearest the panel becomes the default elevator operator. Their job is to prevent the doors from closing while people get on and off.

Open button

開

Close button

閉

NOTE!

The characters for open and close are very similar! Just remember that the character for "open" has two horizontal lines in the center.

If you find yourself as the elevator operator, people may announce their floor to you and expect you to press the button. They will say the number (see p. 16) followed by the suffix -kai.

- First floor: ikkai [ee-Ø-ky]
- Second floor: nikai [nee-ky]
- Third floor: sankai [sahn-ky]

Floor

階

kai

[ky]

NOTE!

Some buildings, especially hospitals, don't have a fourth floor because the number four is considered bad luck.

Depachika

Lower levels in department stores are home to a variety of food shops selling sweet and savory treats of all kinds. These levels are called depachika, literally "department store basement."

Department store

デパート

depâto
[day-pah-ah-toh]

Food level

デパ地下

depachika
[day-pah-chee-kah]

Bag searches

Most public places don't require a bag search to enter. A few government sites do, however, including the Imperial Palace Gardens and the Metropolitan Government Building observation deck.

SELF-SERVICE SHOPS

You've decided to stop by a café or cafeteria. You spot an open table, but by the time you've ordered a drink, selected your snack, and paid, someone else has taken your seat!

The solution? Before you even grab a tray, claim a spot by setting your bag or phone at the table. When you return with your goodies, your valuables will still be there and you'll have a place to sit.

Purses and jackets

In most establishments, especially those with a genkan (see p. 49), placing your things on the floor is considered poor form. Coat racks, baskets, and hooks under the table are provided for you to store your things. It's yet another manifestation of the Japanese penchant for cleanliness.

Ryokan

If you're staying in a ryokan, a traditional inn, you'll be given a yukata, a cotton kimono. When you return to the hotel for the night, change into it (keeping your underclothes on) and feel free to wear it even in the common areas.

Credit: 663highland

HOW TO WEAR A **YUKATA IN A RYOKAN**

Illustrations: Wilfrid Desachy

Put on the yukata.

Wrap the right panel to your left side, covering as much of your torso as possible, then wrap the left panel to your right side. The yukata shouldn't twist and should reach your ankles.

Hold the yukata closed. Wrap the belt two or three times, around the waist for women and around the hips for men.

Knot the belt. The knot can be worn in the front or back.

NOTE!

The left panel always goes over the right panel. The opposite method is only used to dress the dead.

CLOTHING

You'll almost certainly be buying clothing during your trip, whether it's a souvenir T-shirt, extra socks, or something new for the wardrobe back home!

SIZE CONVERSIONS 

NOTE!
Since only 4% of Japanese people are obese, you'll have a hard time finding larger sizes. If there's a chance you won't be able to find your size in Japan, make sure you bring enough clothing for the trip.

NOTE!
Japanese people as a whole tend to be shorter and more slender than Americans, which is evident even in their so-called standard "international" sizes. You may want to try on a larger size than you normally wear (medium instead of small or extra large instead of large).

WOMEN 

Japan	3	5	7	9	11	13	15	17	19	21	23
US	0	2	4	6	8	10	12	14	16	18	20
Universal	XXS	XS	S	S-M	M-L	L	XL	XL-XXL	XL-XXL	XXL	XXL

BRAS 

Japanese bras follow European sizes. The number refers to the band size. The most common cup sizes are the same in both sizing systems.

NOTE!
If in doubt, ask an employee to take your measurements.

Japan	A65	A70	B75	C80	D85	E90
US	30A	32A	34A	36B	38C	40DD/E

MEN 

Shirts

Japanese shirts tend to be cut pretty slim. If you've got a bit of a belly, go a size up.

Japan	S	M	L	XL	XXL
US	14	15	15.5	16.5	17.5

Pants

Japan	29/S	30/M	31/L	32/XL	34	36	38
US	29	30	31	32	34	36	38
Universal	XS	S	M	M–L	L	XL	XXL

CHILDREN 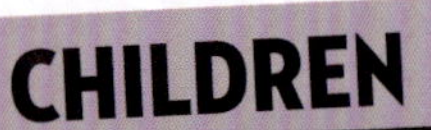

Children's clothes are sized by the child's height in centimeters.

Japan	50–70	70	80	90	95	100	110	120	130	140	150
US	0–6 months	6–12 months	12 months	24 months	36 months	3–4 years	5–6 years	7–8 years	9–10 years	11–12 years	12–14 years

SHOES 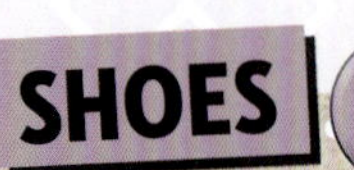

Japanese shoe sizes are based on the length of the foot in centimeters.

Japan	21.5	22	22.5	23	23.5	24	24.5	25	25.5	26	26.5	27	27.5	28	28.5	29
US Men					6	6.5	7–7.5	7.5	8–8.5	9	9–9.5	10–10.5	10.5–11	11–11.5	11.5–12.5	12–13
US Women	4.5–5	5–5.5	6	6.5	7	7.5–8	8–8.5	8.5–9	9.5–10	10–10.5	10–11	11–11.5	11.5–12			

Credit: Teo Romera

MAJOR **CHAINS**

When shopping for clothes, check out chain stores first. They carry a wider range of sizes and often have English-speaking employees to serve tourists. Some even waive the 10% sales tax for tourists (see p. 47).

(see p. 47)

The most popular chains are:

Uniqlo
(market leader)

GU
(sister company with discount prices)

Wego

Shimamura

しまむら

Honeys

Honeys

TRYING ON CLOTHES

At the fitting rooms, an employee will ask you how many items you have and point you to a fitting room.

Women will be offered a gauzy full-face hood to prevent makeup from transferring to clothing.

Take off your shoes before entering the fitting room. There will be a small genkan (see p. 49) just outside, where you should leave your shoes, pointing away from the fitting room.

(see p. 49)

Try on the clothes.

Take everything with you when leaving the fitting room. Return unwanted items to an employee or replace them on the rack yourself.

> **TIP!**
> Endcaps feature bins containing clearance items. Take a moment to browse them. You might find larger sizes, usually heavily discounted. 古着, furugi [foo-roo-ghee] means secondhand clothing.

THRIFT STORES

There are countless thrift stores in Tokyo selling secondhand clothing. The items are often like new, having been worn only once or twice, as Japanese people like to refresh their wardrobe regularly. Most thrift stores are located in fashion districts (see p. 130).

(see p. 130)

Mode Off is a vintage clothing retailer with dozens of locations in Tokyo.

I am looking for___.

... を探しています.

... wo sagashite imasu.
[___ oh sah-gah-shee-tay ee-mahss]

Do you have this in a larger size?

もう少し大きい
のありませんか？

Mō sukoshi ookii no arimasen ka ?
[moh-oh soo-koh-shee oh-oh-kee-ee noh ah-lee-mah-sen kah]

Do you have this in a smaller size?

もう少し小さい
のありませんか？

Mō sukoshi chiisai no arimasen ka ?
[moh-oh soo-koh-shee chee-ee-sy no ah-lee-mah-sen kah]

Do you have this in a longer size?

もう少し長い
のありませすか？

Mō sukoshi nagai no arimasu ka?
[moh-oh soo-koh-shee nah-guy no ah-lee-mah-sen kah]

Do you have this in a shorter size?

もう少し短い
のありますか？

Mō sukoshi mijikai no arimasu ka?
[moh-oh soo-koh-shee mee-jee-ky no ah-lee-mah-sen kah]

Out of stock

売り切れ

urikire
[oo-lee-kee-lay]

Fitting room

試着室 (しちゃくしつ)

shichakushitsu
[shee-cha-koo-shee-tsoo]

Fitting room

ドレッシングルーム

dressing room
[doh-ray-Ø-shin-goo roo-oo-moo]

TRASH

The streets of Tokyo are pristine.
Follow these rules to help keep them that way.

Credit: elmimmo

TRASH

Trash
ゴミ
gomi
[go-mee]

Trash can
ゴミ箱
gomibako
[go-mee-bah-koh]

Recycling is an ingrained habit in Japan. Waste is usually sorted into three major categories.

Flammable trash
Paper, wood, food, cloth, etc.
燃えるゴミ
moerugomi
[moh-ay-roo-go-mee]

Nonflammable trash
Plastic food packaging, bottles, ceramic, glass, etc.
燃えないゴミ
moenaigomi
[moh-ay-ny-go-mee]

Recyclable trash
Paper, cardboard, plastic bottles, cans, etc.
資源ゴミ
shigengomi
[shee-ghen-go-mee]

NOTE!

If you're staying with a local or at an Airbnb, you should see a trash pickup calendar posted somewhere. Whatever you do, don't put out the wrong bin on the wrong day!

PUBLIC TRASH CANS

Public trash cans emphasize recycling. Here are the types of recycling bins you'll see, usually labeled in English.

Newspapers
新聞
shinbun
[sheen-boon]

Magazines
雑誌
zasshi
[zah-Ø-shee]

Metal Cans
カン
kan
[kahn]

Glass bottles
びん or ビン
bin
[been]

Plastic bottles
ペットボトル
PET bottles
[pet-toh bo-too-roo]

Other waste
その他のゴミ
sonohoka no gomi
[so-no-ho-kah no go-mee]

TIP!

You can drop off empty bottles at any vending machine. The slots for plastic bottles and metal cans frequently lead to the same bin. The purpose of the separate slots is to encourage the habit of sorting recyclables at home.

NOTE!

Plastic bags used to be free, but as of July 2020, stores are required to charge for them—an environmental initiative that began ahead of the Olympics.

When to toss your trash

Since the 1995 sarin gas attack in Tokyo, public trash cans have been few and far between. Carry a bag to collect your trash until you find a place to dispose of it. There are three major places to find trash cans:

Train/subway platforms

There are always trash cans on the platforms, so take advantage of them while you wait.

Konbini

Although they are generally reserved for customer use, you can toss your trash in one of their bins, especially if it's outside.

Department stores

You'll see trash cans along the walkways, especially on lower levels where the food vendors are.

TOBACCO

NOTE!

It is illegal to smoke while walking in the street. Doing so risks a fine of ¥2,000. Since April 2020, it has also been illegal to smoke near places frequented by children (schools, plazas, etc.).

Tobacco
たばこ
tabako
[tah-bah-koh]

Large smoking areas are available near major train stations.

Smoking area
喫煙所
kitsuensho
[kee-tsoo-en-sho]

You'll also find cigarette receptacles outside some konbini and near cigarette machines.

Pocket ashtray
携帯灰皿
keitai haizara
[kay-ee-ty hah-ee-zah-rah]

TIP!

Invest in a pocket ashtray. That way you have a place to put the butt when you're done, even if there are no trash cans nearby.

Credit: Asacyan

Indoor smoking is more acceptable in Japan than in the USA. Some malls offer smoking areas, usually near the restrooms.

In July 2020, a law was passed requiring restaurants larger than 100 m² to be completely smoke-free or to provide a separate smoking area. Smaller restaurants (that is, half the restaurants in Tokyo) may allow smoking, as is the case with many izakaya (see p. 80).

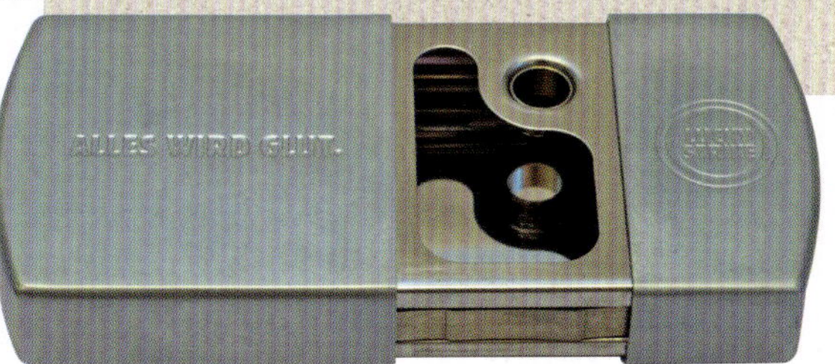

Credit: El Grafo

TIP!

Despite the powerful tobacco lobbies and availability of cheap cigarettes in Japan, your trip may be an opportunity for you to quit. Japanese cigarette brands (Mevius, Seven Stars) come in a range of nicotine concentrations from 1 (lowest) to 10 (highest). If so desired, you could work your way down the scale during your stay and return home with a carton of level 1 cigarettes purchased at the airport duty-free store—the last packs you'll ever smoke.

You might encounter cigarette machines, especially in smoking areas at malls. However, making a purchase requires a Taspo pass, which are only issued to Japanese citizens age 20 and older. That means you won't be able to make a purchase from the machines unless you find a fellow smoker to help you out.

Credit: Byron Villegas

PUBLIC **BATHS**

Public baths are a part of daily life in Japan and have survived the advent of modern plumbing. The activity has as much to do with socializing as hygiene.

SENTŌ **VS. ONSEN**

There are two types of baths in Japan:

Onsen

The hot water comes from natural springs and by law must be 77°F or hotter and contain a certain concentration of minerals. Onsen baths are often located outdoors.

Sentō

Running water is heated before arriving at the bath, which is located in an enclosed room often decorated with a mural of Mount Fuji.

Regardless of which you choose, the goal is to enjoy a moment of relaxation.

Credit: Tzuhsun Hsu

BEFORE GETTING IN

Since you'll be sharing the bath with other people, you don't want to pollute the water with your own grime. Bathe before you get in.

Find an empty stool and shower. Soap up and scrub with the washcloth provided.

Fill the bucket with water and rinse. Make sure to also rinse your bathing area of any traces of soap.

TIP!

If you have long hair, put it up. It should not touch the bath water.

Credit: CMoi

ENTERING **A SENTŌ**

Sentō are marked by an icon consisting of three wisps of steam rising from a bath. You can also spot the baths from a distance by the steam coming out of the vent.

Baths are generally an activity undertaken at the end of the day, but most public baths are open from 7 a.m. to 2 a.m.

Remove your shoes in the genkan and place them in a locker.

Pay at the desk. Rates are set annually by the city based on the cost of a bowl of noodles and are the same throughout Tokyo. In 2021, the price of admission was ¥480 for adults and ¥180 for children.

If you didn't bring a towel, you can rent one. Always rent a washcloth.

In the main hall, the blue curtains lead to the area for men and the red curtains to the area for women.

Once in the changing room, strip down completely. This includes necklaces, bracelets, and rings. The key to your locker comes on a stretchy wristband for you to wear.

Exit the changing room to the bath area. You'll go back through the changing room on the way out.

GETTING **IN**

Bath temperatures range from about 99°F to 106°F. Use the long-handled pitcher at the edge of the bath to scoop bath water and pour it across your shoulders and body to acclimate yourself to the water temperature.

Climb into the bath and relax. Baths usually last between 15 and 30 minutes.

NOTE!

Never put your head under the water. Similarly, never dip your towel in the water. Leave it at the edge of the bath or wrap it around your head.

NOTE!

The heat can cause dizziness. If you feel the slightest bit unwell, get out and take a cool shower.

Be extra careful if you have a heart condition.

Some sentō also offer cold water baths to stimulate blood circulation, Jacuzzis, or even saunas (sometimes for an extra fee). Anytime you switch to a different bath, use the bucket in the shower area to rinse off.

TIP!

Chat with your fellow bathers! Public baths used to only be available near temples and served as a place to catch up on the latest local gossip. This social aspect has continued to endure. There's even a Japanese saying that goes, "All are equal when naked." In a public bath, bosses and employees can chat as equals. It may be your only opportunity to mingle with real locals, despite the language barrier.

GETTING **OUT**

Once you're clean and relaxed from the bath, get out and dry off with your towel.

Back in the changing room, you'll find sinks, mirrors, and hair dryers. Men often shave here, although some prefer to do it in the shower. For women, it's an opportunity to reapply makeup if desired.

TIP!

Most sentō also offer a scale. You can see if you've lost any weight on your Japanese diet!

Toss your used washcloth (and bath towel, if you rented one) into the hamper and get dressed at your locker.

Thank the person at the front desk and retrieve your shoes.

After sweating in the bath, it's a good idea to rehydrate. Vending machines are everywhere, perhaps even in the sentō, offering favorite beverages for Japanese adults (beer) and children (milk).

Credit: Travis

TATTOOS

Despite encouragement from the government to eliminate this old-fashioned custom, many onsen ban tattoos, which have traditionally been associated with the Japanese Mafia (yakuza). Sentō tend to have more relaxed rules, but you should still ask ahead of time.

Or visit Tattoo Friendly at https://tattoo-friendly.jp to see which establishments allow tattoos.

AIR-CONDITIONING

You'll find that all hotels include air conditioning. But how does that darned remote control work?

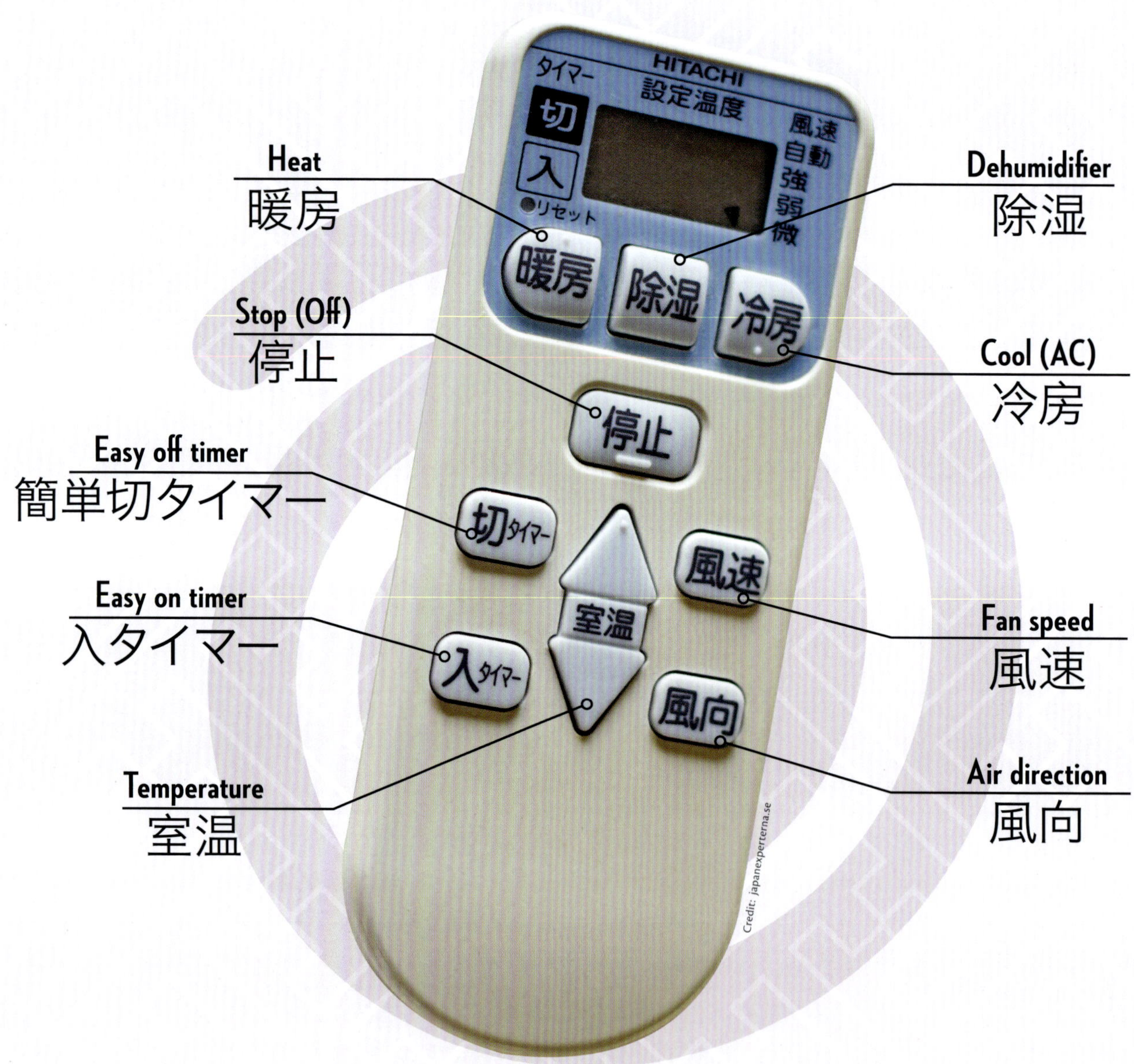

Heat
暖房

Dehumidifier
除湿

Stop (Off)
停止

Cool (AC)
冷房

Easy off timer
簡単切タイマー

Easy on timer
入タイマー

Fan speed
風速

Temperature
室温

Air direction
風向

LOST AND FOUND

You forgot your purse under a bench or your wallet fell out of your pocket. What do you do now?

STEP 1

Retrace your steps. In most cases, you'll find the item right where you left it. If you don't see it right away, look around. Someone might have placed it on a nearby ledge or bench, out of harm's way.

Head back to the last place you know you had the item (restaurant, mall) and ask for help. If you still can't find it, move on to Step 2.

STEP 2

If you can't find the lost item yourself, go to the nearest kōban.

Talk to the agent on duty. They will take down details on the item:

- Size
- Color
- When you lost it
- Where you lost it

Police station

交番

kōban
[koh-oh-bahn]

Japanese people will almost always turn in found valuables (laptops, wallets, ID cards) to kōban.

With a little luck, someone will have turned in your belongings and the police can return them to you.

If not, fill out a form with a phone number where you can be reached.

TIP!

Slip the business card for your hotel into your wallet, purse, and Pocket Wi-Fi pouch, and tape it to your phone. If your item is turned in at a kōban, police will call the hotel and deliver the item.

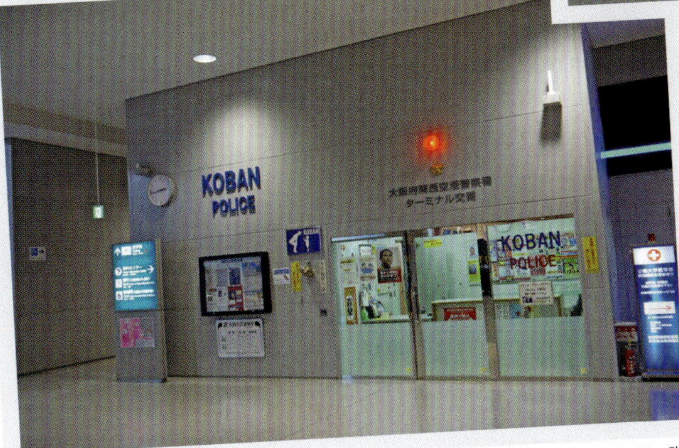

WHAT IS **A KŌBAN** ?

Kōban are neighborhood police stations. They handle local complaints (noisy drunks, spats between neighbors, lost pets).

They're also the best friend of lost tourists, both Japanese and otherwise. They can point you in the right direction.

Credit: ChingHua Chung

KEY WORDS AND PHRASES

GREETINGS AND ETIQUETTE

Good morning
おはよう ございます
Ohayō gozaimasu
[oh-hah-yo-oh go-zah-ee-mass]

Good afternoon
こんにちは
Konnichiwa
[koh-nee-chee-wah]

Good evening
こんばんは
Konbanwa
[kohn-bahn-wah]

Please
お願いします
Onegaishimasu
[oh-nay-gah-ee-shee-mahss]

___ please
___ ください
___ kudasai
[___ koo-dah-sy]

Thanks
ありがとう
Arigatō
[ah-lee-gah-toh]

Thank you
ありがとうございます
Arigatō gozaimasu
[ah-lee-gah-toh go-zah-ee-mass]

Thank you very much
どうもありがとう ございます
Dōmo arigatō gozaimasu
[doh-moh ah-lee-gah-toh go-zah-ee-mahss]

Pardon me
すみません
Sumimasen
[soo-mee-mah-sen]

I'm sorry
ごめんなさい
Gomen nasai
[go-men nah-sy]

Pardon me, may I take photos?
すみません, 写真を撮ってもいいですか?
Sumimasen, shashin wo tottemo ii desuka ?
[soo-mee-mah-sen sha-sheen oh toh-Ø-tay-moh ee-ee day-ska]

Pardon me, may I photograph you?
すみません、あなたの写真を撮ってもいいですか?
Sumimasen, anata no shashin wo tottemo ii desuka ?
[soo-mee-mah-sen ah-nah-tah no sha-sheen oh toh-Ø-tay-moh ee-ee day-ska]

ELEVATOR

Open button
開

Close button
閉

Floor
階
kai
[ky]

Yen
円
en
[en]

MONEY

How much is this?
これはいくらですか ？
Kore wa ikura desu ka ?
[koh-lay wah ee-koo-rah day-soo kah]

Change
お釣り
otsuri
[oh-tsoo-ree]

Money
お金
okane
[oh-kah-nay]

SHOPPING

I'm looking for___.
___を探しています
___wo sagashite imasu.
[___ oh sah-gah-shee-tay ee-mahss]

Out of stock
売り切れ
urikire
[oo-lee-kee-lay]

Souvenir gifts
お土産
omiyage
[oh-mee-yah-gay]

Umbrella
傘
kasa
[kah-sah]

Bag
鞄
kaban
[kah-bahn]

Cell phone
携帯
keitai
[kay-ee-ty]

Smartphone
スマーフォ
sumāfo
[soo-mah-ah-fo]

Clothing
服
fuku
[foo-koo]

T-shirt
ティーシャツ
tīshatsu
[tee-shah-tsoo]

Pants
ズボン
zubon
[tzoo-bohn]

Skirt
スカート
sukāto
[soo-kah-ah-toh]

Dress
ワンピース
wanpīsu
[wahn-pee-ee-soo]

Shoes
靴
kutsu
[koo-tsoo]

Socks
靴下
kutsushita
[koo-tsoo-shee-tah]

Underclothes
下着
shitagi
[shee-tah-ghee]

Coat
上着
uwagi
[oo-wah-ghee]

Hat
帽子
bōshi
[bo-oh-shee]

Kimono
着物
kimono
[kee-moh-noh]

Yukata
浴衣
yukata
[yoo-kah-tah]

Fitting room (1)
試着室 (しちゃくしつ)
shichakushitsu
[shee-cha-koo-shee-tsoo]

Fitting room (2)
ドレッシングルーム
dressing room
[doh-ray-Ø-shin-goo roo-oo-moo]

Do you have this in a larger size?
もう少し大きいのありませんか？
Mō sukoshi ookii no arimasen ka ?
[moh-oh soo-koh-shee oh-oh-kee-ee no ah-lee-mah-sen kah]

Do you have this in a smaller size?
もう少し小さいのありませんか？
Mō sukoshi chiisai no arimasen ka ?
[moh-oh soo-koh-shee chee-ee-sy no ah-lee-mah-sen kah]

Do you have this in a longer size?
もう少し長いのありますか？
Mō sukoshi nagai no arimasu ka ?
[moh-oh soo-koh-shee nah-guy no ah-lee-mah-sen kah]

Do you have this in a shorter size?
もう少し短いのありますか？
Mō sukoshi mijikai no arimasu ka ?
[moh-oh soo-koh-shee mee-jee-ky no ah-lee-mah-sen kah]

TRASH

Trash
ゴミ
gomi
[go-mee]

Pocket ashtray
携帯灰皿
keitai haizara
[kay-ee-ty hah-ee-zah-rah]

Trash can
ゴミ箱
gomibako
[go-mee-bah-ko]

Smoking area
喫煙所
kitsuensho
[kee-tsoo-en-sho]

LOST AND FOUND

Police station
交番
kōban
[koh-oh-bahn]

I lost ___.
___をなくしてしまいました。
wo nakushite shimaimashita
[_______ oh nah-koo-shee-tay shee-my-mah-shee-tah]

RESTROOMS

Bathroom
トイレ
toire
[toh-ee-lay]

Restroom
(more polite)
お手洗い
otearai
[oh-tay-ah-lye]

Where is the bathroom?
トイレはどこですか？
Toire wa doko desuka ?
[toh-ee-lay wah doh-koh day-ska]

Where are the restrooms?
(more polite)
お手洗いはどこですか？
Otearai wa doko desuka ?
[oh-tay-ah-lay wah doh-koh day-ska]

PUBLIC BATHS

Hot springs
温泉
onsen
[ohn-sen]

Public baths
銭湯
sentō
[sen-toh-oh]

Shower gel
ボディーソープ
body soap
[bo-dee soh-oh-poo]

Shampoo
シャンプー
shampoo
[shahn-poo-oo]

Men
男
otoko
[oh-toh-koh]

Women
女
onna
[ohn-nah]

Towel
タオル
taoru
[tah-oh-loo]

Bath
お風呂
ofuro
[oh-foo-ro]

DINING

MEALS: AN OVERVIEW

Japanese cuisine includes an enormous range of foods and dishes, but here is what a typical meal might look like.

THE JAPANESE TYPICALLY EAT THREE MEALS A DAY

BREAKFAST

A typical Japanese breakfast consists of a bowl of rice, miso soup, and various traditional or Western-inspired accompaniments:

- Grilled fish
- Raw, fried, or hardboiled egg or omelet
- Nattō (fermented soybean)
- Buttered toast
- Fruit (or fruit juice)
- Coffee
- Sausage

Credit: bryan...

Typical hours: 8 a.m.–10 a.m.

Café chains (Excelsior, Doutor, Starbucks, St. Marc) offer Western-style options. Denny's has longer breakfast hours, 6 a.m. to 11 a.m.

LUNCH

Lunch is often eaten on the go or during a lunch break. It consists of a single course accompanied by a bottle of water, tea, or beer.

Bento: A lunch set brought from home or purchased from a local mini-mart

Ramen: Noodle bowl

Donburi: Rice bowl with toppings

Typical hours: 11 a.m.–1 p.m.

Credit: Abendstrom

NOTE!
Most restaurants are busy during lunchtime. You should leave as soon as you're finished eating.

TIP!
If you really want to linger over dessert and/or coffee, go to a chain café (Doutor, Starbucks, Tully's). Many Europeans love the espresso at Excelsior.

DINNER

Dinner most resembles what Westerners think of as a stereotypical Japanese meal. The Japanese eat around the same time as Americans (6 p.m.), but some restaurants, particularly izakaya, are open late.

Typical hours: 5 p.m.–8 p.m.
Izakaya: 5 p.m.–midnight

(see p. 80)

Credit: Emma Haruka Iwao

NOTE!
Itadakimasu [ee-tah-dah-kee-mass] doesn't mean "Bon appétit" or "Let's eat." Rather, it's an expression of gratitude for the person who made the meal. Direct it at the chef rather than at your dining companions.

Credit: niconico0

THE ESSENTIALS OF JAPANESE DINING

WHITE RICE

White rice is ubiquitous and so important to Japanese cuisine that the word for it, gohan, is the same word for a meal.

Credit: Marco Verch

TIP!
Don't pour soy sauce onto white rice.

SOY SAUCE

Use it sparingly and don't waste it.

Credit: Tim Reckmann

DASHI STOCK

The Japanese equivalent of chicken stock but usually made from dried fish and seaweed. The vegetarian version, shōjin dashi [sho-jin dah-shee], is made of konbu and shiitake mushrooms.

MISO SOUP

Miso soup
味噌汁
misoshiru
[mee-soh-shee-roo]

Made of fermented soybean paste (miso) and dashi stock and garnished with seaweed, tofu, and sesame seeds.

Credit: Adonis Chen from Taiwan 台北市賣陽街二段 三味食堂

TEA

Green tea
お茶
ocha
[oh-cha]

Matcha tea
抹茶
matcha
[mah-cha]

Mugi tea
麦茶
mugicha
[moo-ghee-cha]

Black tea
紅茶
koocha
[koo-cha]

Oolong tea
烏龍茶
ūroncha
[oo-lohn-cha]

- Ocha [oh-cha] お茶 is the general word for tea but also refers to sencha green tea, which can be served cold or hot but never sweetened.
- Matcha [mah-cha] 抹茶 is a powdered green tea.
- Mugi tea (mugicha) 麦茶 is made from barley.
- The term for black tea (koocha) 紅茶 actually translates to "red tea."
- Oolong tea (ūroncha) 烏龍茶 has more caffeine and is also very popular.

RESTAURANTS: AN OVERVIEW

The city of Tokyo alone has more restaurants than the entire states of California and New York combined (150,000 vs. 135,000)! Japanese restaurant etiquette depends on the size and type of establishment, but here are some commonalities.

CHOOSING A RESTAURANT

Credit: Azchael

Around 11 a.m. or 12 p.m., look around to see which restaurants have the longest lines, an indicator of the best restaurants. Alternatively, look for ones with mostly mothers and kids, another indicator.

NOTE!

Sandwich boards on the sidewalk may be advertisements for restaurants upstairs, not on the ground floor. Look for a floor number (for example, 2F or 3F) or a staircase icon.

TIP!

Some restaurants offer tabehōdai [tah-bay-hoh-oh-dye] 食べ放, all-you-can-eat options lasting 90 or 120 minutes. They usually serve a single specialty (barbecue, shabu-shabu, shish kebabs, sushi), not a varied buffet.

PARTY SIZE

Upon entering, you'll hear "Irasshaimase!" which means "welcome." The employee will ask "Nanmeisama deshoka?" meaning "How many?"

Respond with the appropriate number (see p. 93) followed by the suffix -mei [may].

For example, a party of four would be "yonmei desu."

TIP!

The Japanese starts off familiar. Stick out your index finger to mean one, add the middle finger to mean two, the ring finger for three, the pinkie finger for four, and the thumb for five.

But for six, stick out an index finger of one hand and place it against the open palm of the other hand. Add the middle finger for seven, the ring finger for eight, and the pinkie for nine. For ten, you'll end up with an open palm facing away from you and another open palm placed against it facing you.

SMOKING OR NONSMOKING

Many restaurants, including fast-food places, still offer smoking sections. You'll very likely be asked "Kitsuen seki to kinen seki, dochiraga yoroshiideshōka?" ("Smoking or non?").

Smoking	Nonsmoking
喫煙席	禁煙席
kitsuen seki	kinen seki
[kee-tsoo-en say-kee]	[kee-nen say-kee]

NOTE!

The question might also be phrased as "Do you smoke?" ("Otabako wa oshini nararemasuka?").

ORDERING

After you're seated, you'll be given a wet towel (oshibori) to clean your hands.

NOTE!
The towel is for your hands only, not your face.

Once you've decided on your order, press the button at your table to call the server. If there isn't one, you can raise your hand and call out "Sumimasen!"

I'd like to order
注文をお願いします
Chūmon wo onegaishimasu
[choo-oo-mon oh oh-nay-gah-ee-shee-mahss]

Point to the menu to order. If you'd like more than one of something, indicate the number with your fingers as instructed above.

When you're done ordering, say "Ijou de" [ee-jo-oh day], meaning "That's all."

If you think you might order something later, say "Toriaezu ijou de" [toh-ree-ah-ay-zoo ee-jo-oh day], meaning "That's all for now." The server will read back your order to make sure it's correct and then bring it out to you.

TIP!
Some restaurants display sanpuru, extremely realistic plastic models of their dishes, in the front window. Take a picture of the one you want to order so you can show it to the server.

TIP!
If you're not sure what to order, ask for the chef's recommendation.

Chef's recommendation
お勧めは？
Osusume wa ?
[oh-soo-soo-may wah]

WAIT TIMES

There might be a wait time depending on the restaurant and time of day. The server will tell you the approximate wait time. If it'll be more than 15 minutes, you can kill time walking around and then come back. The estimates are sometimes accurate down to the minute!

NOTE!
Some restaurants conduct the entire transaction via machine. Most of these have a menu in English. If not, ask an employee.

ASKING FOR **THE CHECK**

Get the server's attention by calling out "Sumimasen!" and ask for the check:

Check, please
お会計をお願いします
Okaikei wo onegaishimasu
[oh-ky-kay oh oh-nay-gah-ee-shee-mahss]

TIP!
If you catch the server's eye, you can also cross your index fingers in the shape of an X. This is the sign for "Check, please" in Japan.

NOTE!
Near closing time, the server will announce last call, your last chance to place an order.

PAY
THE BILL

Don't tip! The Japanese are proud of their good service, and a tip undermines that.

SHOES

Some restaurants require customers to remove their shoes (see p. 49). Store your shoes in one of the lockers, which usually have a numbered key. The more traditional restaurants use wooden keys with numbers written in kanji—a test of your Japanese language skills!

THANK
THE STAFF

Say "Gochisōsama!" [goh-chee-soh-oh-ah-mah] to express appreciation for the meal.

CHOPSTICKS

Although plenty of Westerners know how to use chopsticks, many are still unaware of the etiquette surrounding them in Japan.

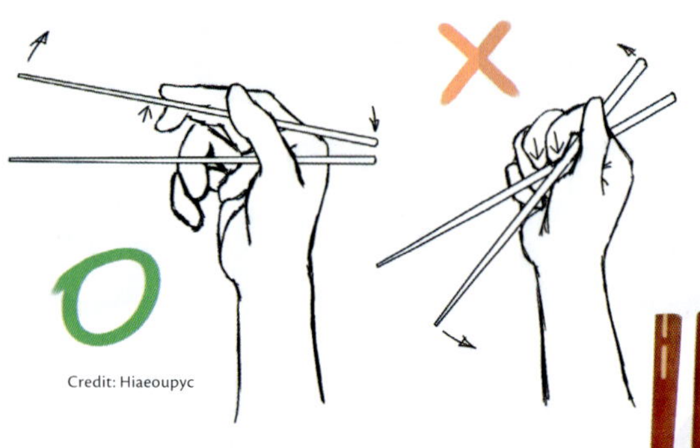

Credit: Hiaeoupyc

HOW TO **HOLD CHOPSTICKS**

Balance one chopstick in the valley between your thumb and forefinger and on your ring finger. This chopstick will not move.

Hold the other chopstick with the tips of your thumb, index, and middle finger like a pen. This chopstick will move to pick up food.

CHOPSTICK **FAUX PAS**

In Japan, always abide by these two cardinal chopstick rules:

Never leave your chopsticks stabbed vertically into a bowl of rice (or any other food).

Two people should never hold the same piece of food at the same time. If you want to pass a piece of food to someone, place it on their plate and let them pick it up.

These two gestures are performed only at funerals and thus are inappropriate at the table.

Credit: Jeanne Bucher

TIP!
Here's how to turn your chopstick wrapper into a chopstick rest.

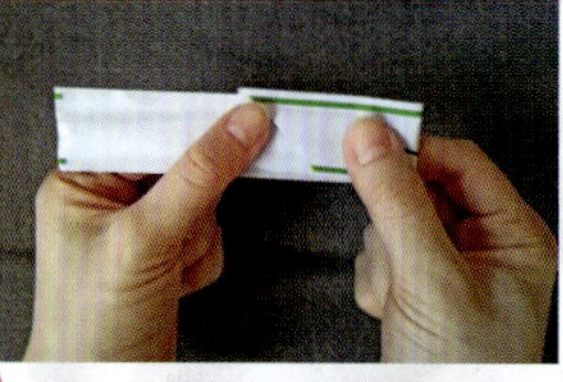

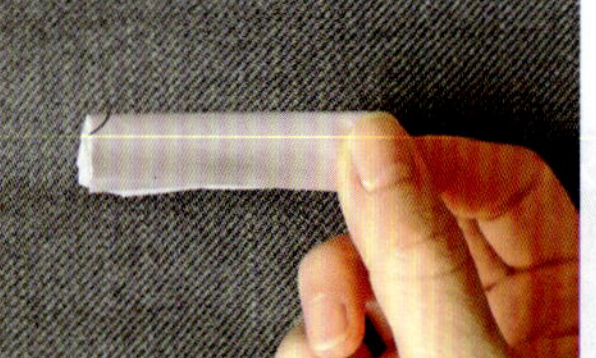

Credit: Jeanne Bucher

WHERE TO PUT YOUR CHOPSTICKS

- Never rest your chopsticks on the edge of a bowl or plate. You should have been given a chopstick rest. If not, it's because you've been given waribashi, disposable chopsticks connected at the top.

- To use waribashi, break them apart. Make sure to do this at lap level to avoid accidentally elbowing the person next to you.

- Don't rub the chopsticks together to get rid of splinters. It implies to the chef that the wood is poor quality.

- Lay the chopsticks flat on their wrapper.

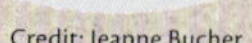

Credit: Jeanne Bucher

TIP!
Chefs in smaller restaurants LOVE this type of attention to etiquette by gaijin—so much so that you might get a small glass of free sake at the end of your meal!

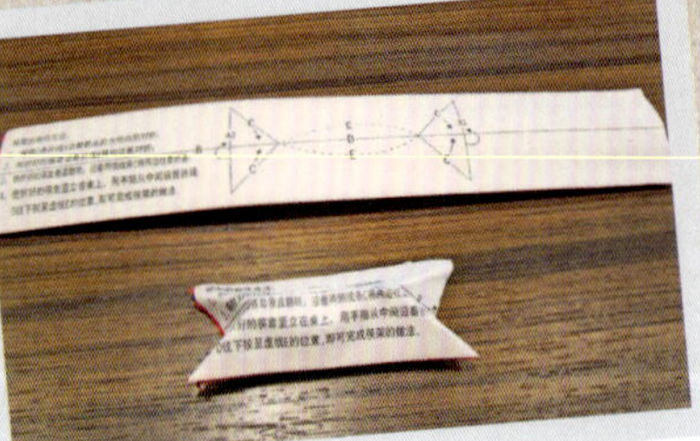

Credit: Micah Sittig

BASIC **RULES**

There are more than forty faux pas you could make with chopsticks, so no matter what, you're likely to commit one or two.

Nevertheless, here are some basic rules that every Japanese child knows.

Never point at someone with your chopsticks. You wouldn't do it with a knife, so don't do it with chopsticks. Avoid pointing in general, even with your finger (see p. 51).

Don't use chopsticks with one in each hand.

Credit: Jeanne Bucher

If you pick up food from a shared platter, don't put it back.

Don't stab your food to eat it.

Only use one end of the chopsticks. Don't flip them around and use the other end to take from shared platters.

Don't use your chopsticks to push dishes or plates around.

Don't hold food higher than mouth level.

When taking food from a shared platter, place it on your plate before eating it.

Don't bite off a piece of food from your chopsticks. Put the whole thing in your mouth. Food is precut into bite-size pieces.

EATING **WITHOUT CHOPSTICKS**

If you don't know how to use chopsticks, don't worry. There are lots of things you can eat with your hands (sushi, shish kabobs, onigiri) or spoons (curry rice, omu rice).

Then again, don't be afraid to ask for a fork, spoon, or knife.

TIP!
You can buy travel chopsticks at any 100-yen shop (see p. 104) to carry with you.

LOCAL SPECIALTIES

Japanese cuisine comes in many varieties. The etiquette differs for each type.

SUSHI

There are several ways to enjoy sushi, the crown jewel of Japanese cuisine: at traditional restaurants, at conveyor belt diners, or as a grab-and-go meal.

The main types of sushi are:

Sushi: A ball of rice (shari) with some kind of topping (neta). The official term is nigirisushi.

Sashimi: Slices of raw fish.

Makisushi: Seaweed topped with rice and other ingredients, rolled up, and sliced.

Credit: Peterjhpark

Credit: Lord Mountbatten

Credit: Phengphian Laogumnerd Cuisine

NOTE!

Not all sushi is made with raw fish. Fillings may be cooked (eel, shrimp) or may not even be seafood at all (egg, eggplant, tofu).

CONDIMENTS

Soy sauce

醤油

shōyu

[sho-oh-yoo]

The Japanese are respectful toward soy sauce—an essential ingredient in their cuisine—so don't waste it. Pour just a dash into your sauce dish. Don't fill it all the way; you can always take more later. It's better than leaving leftovers at the end of the meal.

Credit: Tim Reckmann

NOTE!

Dip your sushi into the soy sauce fish side down. The soy sauce should enhance the sushi, not overpower it, which it will if you dip the rice in the sauce.

Wasabi

山葵

wasabi

[wah-sah-bee]

Wasabi looks like green modeling clay and tastes similar to horseradish. Eat it only with sashimi. Sushi will have been seasoned by the chef.

Credit: june29

NOTE!

Don't mix wasabi into your soy sauce. Place a small amount on top of the sashimi, then dip the underside in soy sauce.

Pickled ginger

ガリ

gari

[gah-lee]

Eat a piece of pickled ginger between bites of sushi to cleanse the palate.

TO **SUM UP**

- Pour a small amount of soy sauce into the sauce dish.

- If desired, place a small amount of wasabi on top of your sashimi.

- Dip sushi into soy sauce fish side down.

- Sushi should be eaten in one bite.

- Eat a piece of ginger between bites.

KAITENZUSHI

(Conveyer belt sushi)

At conveyor belt sushi diners, feel free to open the boxes and drawers at the table. That's where chopsticks and condiments are kept. If you don't see any wasabi at the table, there will be a bowl on the conveyor belt with packets of it.

Green tea is free. Grab a cup, add a scoop of tea leaves, and press your cup against the button underneath the conveyor belt to dispense the desired amount of hot water.

Each plate color usually indicates a particular price. You can estimate your bill at any time by counting your empty plates.

Credit: Alberto Carrasco Casado

NOODLES

There are three types of noodles in Japan: ramen, udon, and soba. Ramen is by far the most popular. You could call it the peanut butter and jelly sandwich of Japan. Tokyo alone has over 5,000 ramen restaurants!

👍 TIP!

No matter the noodle type, it's OK to slurp them! Unlike in America, slurping is actually polite, an expression of appreciation for the chef. Plus, it cools down hot noodles as you eat them.

RAMEN ラーメン OR らーめん

Ramen are a type of wheat noodle ubiquitous in Japan. Unlike udon and soba, ramen actually came from China.

A standard bowl of ramen includes:

- Broth
- Thin, wavy noodles
- A slice or two of pork
- Green onions
- Seaweed

You can choose to add other toppings, including poached egg (ajitama), corn (corn), butter (butter), extra pork slices (chāshū), bean sprouts (moyashi), or bamboo shoots (menma).

There are four types of broth:

Salt	Soy sauce	Miso	Pork
塩	醤油	味噌	豚骨
shio	shōyu	miso	tonkotsu
[shee-oh]	[sho-oh-yoo]	[mee-soh]	[tohn-koh-tsoo]

Most ramen restaurants offer counter service. Once you've finished eating, return your dishes and chopsticks to the counter.

In many places, food and beverages are ordered at a ticket machine. Insert your coins, make a selection, and retrieve your change. Choose a seat and give your ticket to the server, who will bring you your order (see pp. 72–73).

Most ramen restaurants also offer gyoza and fried pork and green onion dumplings as side dishes.

Credit: Guilhem Vellut

BONUS

Another type of ramen is tsukemen, where thicker noodles are served separately and dipped in broth before eating.

UDON 饂飩 OR うどん

Udon noodles are thicker than ramen noodles and usually served in a lighter broth. There are no standard toppings for udon, just a huge range of selections, although most are pretty healthy (tempura, tofu). Udon noodles are also served stir-fried.

BONUS

Bukkake udon is a variation in which sauce is poured over the noodles.

Credit: Ryosuke Sekido

SOBA 蕎麦 OR そば

Soba noodles are made from buckwheat—great for people going gluten free.

Like udon, soba can be served in a variety of ways, not just in soup.

Credit: m-louis .®

BONUS

A popular summertime dish is zarusoba, soba noodles and sauce served chilled.

TIP!

In Japan, any stir-fried noodle dish is called yakisoba, even if it's made with other noodles.

DONBURI

Donburi is a bowl (don) of hot rice topped with accompaniments.

Gyuudon
beef slices

Katsudon
breaded pork cutlet

Tendon
tempura

Oyakodon
egg and chicken

Credit: Arnaud 25

NOTE!

Chirashi, a bowl of cold, vinegar-seasoned rice topped with cold raw fish, is not considered donburi.

Major chains

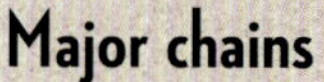

Tendon tenya   Yoshinoya   Matsuya   Sukiya

CURRY RICE

"Curry" is pronounced [kah-lay].

Curry rice consists of chopped vegetables in a thick, spicy gravy served with white rice and your choice of accompaniments.

You can choose the accompaniments (beef, pork, tempura, croquettes), as well as the spice level (generally on a scale of 1 to 10).

- **Chain:** CoCo Ichiban Curry

FRIED FOODS

Tempura

Vegetables or seafood coated with a light batter and deep-fried (similar to fish and chips)

Karaage

Chunks of chicken or octopus coated in a thicker batter and deep-fried (similar to chicken nuggets)

Korokke

Croquettes made of mashed potatoes mixed with ground meat and onions. May also be made with pumpkin, vegetables only, crab, etc.

Tonkatsu

Breaded pork cutlet served with a special sauce

Credit: Ryusei Hosono

OMU RICE

Rice stir-fried with vegetables and chicken and topped with an omelet and demi-glace sauce.

- **Chain:** Rakeru

Credit: Hajime NAKANO

YAKINIKU

Diners grill thinly sliced meat at the table and dip it in a special sauce.

Credit: Matt Biddulph

SHABU-SHABU

Shabu-shabu and sukiyaki are both a style of dining that involves a pot of seasoned meat and vegetable broth simmering at the table.

For best results, first add some of the vegetables and tofu to the broth for flavor.

Dip meat in the broth for ten seconds or so to cook it, then place it on your plate.

Dip the meat in sauce or raw egg and eat it with a mouthful of rice.

Alternate meat with vegetables and tofu. Replace the vegetables in the broth as they finish cooking.

Credit: cyclonebill

IZAKAYA

Izakaya are a cross between a bar and a tapas restaurant. They're a place for office workers to blow off steam, grab a bite, and enjoy a few drinks before heading home.

Credit: foooomio

NOTE!

Many izakaya allow smoking. Restaurants 100 m² or larger must offer a nonsmoking section as well. Ask before being seated.

Once you sit down, you'll be served a small snack or otōshi. This is not like the free baskets of bread at an American restaurant! It is the cost of entry, and you will be billed for it.

Customers are all served the same otōshi, but they are made to order and vary daily. Feel free to ask for something different if you have a food allergy or dietary restrictions. Notify the server as soon as you can.

Izakaya are ultimately a place to unwind. You might end up sitting next to some regulars, in which case you should ask what they recommend.

TIP!

Keep a folder of photos and images on your phone, including a map of your home country with your city marked, to show to Japanese people you meet. You might also want to include pictures of landmarks, dishes, or anything else locals might find unusual or interesting.

Most dishes are made to share. Take from the shared platter and place the food on your plate before eating it.

Dishes served hot

Chicken nuggets
とり唐揚げ

tori karaage
[toh-lee kah-rah-ah-gay]

Octopus balls
たこ焼き

takoyaki
[tah-koh-yah-kee]

fried balls stuffed with octopus

Chicken skewers
焼鳥

yakitori
[yah-kee-toh-lee]

Chicken served on a stick. The name varies depending on how it's cooked.

Chicken balls
捏ね

tsukune
[tsoo-koo-nay]

Chicken breast
四つ身

yotsumi
[yo-tsoo-mee]

With onion
ねぎま/葱間

negima
[nay-ghee-mah]

Thigh
股

momo
[moh-moh]

Liver
レバー

rebā
[lay-bah-ah]

Gizzards
ずり / 砂肝

zuri / sunagimo
[zoo-lee / soo-nah-ghee-moh]

NOTE!

Skewers come in two versions, shio (salty) and tare (sweet). Try them both!

Fried tofu
揚げ出し豆腐

agedashi dōfu
[ah-gay-dah-shee doh-oh-doo]

Fried tofu served in broth

Marinated fish
西京焼き

saikyō yaki
[sy-kee-oh yah-kee]

Fish marinated in miso and grilled

Credit: Leng Cheng

Credit: Lombroso

Stingray fish
エイヒレ
eihire
[ay-hee-ray]

Grilled and served with mayonnaise.

Pizza
ピザ
piza
[pee-zah]

The Japanese have their own version of this Italian classic.

Edamame
枝豆
edamame
[ay-dah-mah-may]

Soybeans served hot or cold. Eat the beans and discard the pods.

Tea rice
お茶漬け
ochazuke
[oh-cha-zoo-kay]

Rice drizzled with green tea or dashi stock and garnished with toppings. A nice light way to end a meal.

Korokke
コロッケ
korokke
[kor-ohk-kay]

Croquettes made of mashed potatoes mixed with ground meat and onions.

Grilled mackerel
鯱
hokke
[hok-kay]

Remove the spine. Eat the flesh using chopsticks.

Rolled omelet
卵焼き
tamagoyaki
[tah-mah-go-yah-kee]

Served hot or cold, sometimes with grated radish (daikon). Place some of the radish onto a bite of egg, add a drop of soy sauce, and enjoy!

Fried dumplings
餃子
gyōza
[ghee-oh-zah]

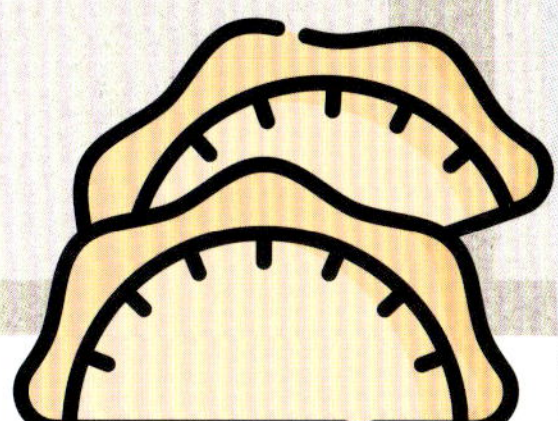

Dishes served cold

Mashed potato salad
ポテトサラダ
potato salad
[po-tay-toh sah-lah-dah]

Mashed potatoes mixed with various raw vegetables (carrot, cucumber, onion) and mayo. Sometimes contains ham. Ask if you're vegetarian.

Fermented soybean
納豆
nattō
[naht-toh-oh]

Fermented soybeans with a strong flavor similar to bleu cheese.

Octopus ceviche with wasabi
たこわさ
takowasa
[tah-koh-wah-sah]

Pickled plum
梅干し
umeboshi
[oo-may-bo-shee]

Horse sashimi
馬刺
basashi
[bah-sah-shee]

Preserved vegetables
漬物
tsukemono
[tah-kay-mo-no]

Sushi/sashimi
寿司/刺身
sushi/sashimi
[soo-shee / sah-shee-mee]

Tofu
豆腐
tōfu
[toh-foo]

Miso eggplant
なす田楽
nasu dengaku
[nah-soo den-gah-koo]

Credit: yamauchi

BEVERAGES

ALCOHOL

Alcohol plays a more important role in Japanese society than you might think. It's the only valid excuse to say what's really on your mind.

NOTE!

You must be age 20 or older to purchase alcohol or tobacco in Japan.

Alcohol abuse is hazardous to your health. Drink responsibly. Smoking kills. It can't be repeated often enough.

NOTE!

Tabehōdai (see p. 72) means "all you can eat." Similarly, many izakaya, bars, and karaoke bars offer nomihōdai (飲み放題), all you can drink.

TIP!

Some places offer both. Nonalcoholic drinks are included in the price.

CUSTOMS

You're hanging out with a group of Japanese people and you're getting along great. Here are some tips on manners to keep the good times rolling.

Never pour your own drink. Make sure to serve your friends, who will do the same for you.

For the first toast, everyone's glass is filled before clinking glasses and shouting "Kanpai!" [kahn-py].

If you don't really want to drink, don't drain your glass. But do take at least a few sips so as not to insult the person who poured it.

The Japanese drink to lower their inhibitions and expect you to do the same. If you don't want to get drunk but also don't want to offend your drinking buddies, tell them you're on medication. It's a little white lie that will prevent a massive hangover the next morning.

NOTE!

Don't say "chin chin" to mean "cheers." It means "penis" in Japanese!

I'm on medication

治療中です

Chiryō chū desu
[chee-ree-yo-oh choo-oo day-soo]

Credit: Shingieun

Credit: David Pursehouse

Credit: Tatsuo Yamashita

Credit: Mj-bird

BEER (5% ABV)

Beer is the most popular alcoholic beverage and also the most highly taxed. The tax rate is based on the malt content. Beverages containing at least 67% malt can legally be called beer or bīru [bee-ee-roo].

At smaller ramen restaurants, beer may be the only beverage on offer other than tea and water.

There are five major brands of beer on the market: Asahi, Kirin, Sapporo, Suntory, and Yebisu.

Draft beer: Nama bīru.

NOTE!

Another type of beer is called happōshu 発泡酒 [hap-poh-oh-shoo], in which malt is replaced with pea or soy protein.

TIP!

If you're unsure whether a can contains beer or soda, look at or feel the top of the can under the lid. Alcoholic beverages feature braille.

SAKE (14%–17% ABV)

TIP!

In Japanese, the word sake simply means any alcoholic beverage. The Japanese word for the rice wine is nihonshu, literally "Japanese alcohol." If you call it sake, no one will think less of you. But if you call it nihonshu, they'll be impressed!

Nihonshu
日本酒
nihonshu
[nee-hon-shoo]

- When served hot, nihonshu comes in a bottle and is poured into tiny cups. Note: Don't drink it like a shot of liquor! Nihonshu is meant to be sipped.
- When served chilled, nihonshu comes in a glass carafe in a wooden box (masu). To make sure your glass is filled all the way, Japanese people will overfill it until it spills. Take a few sips, then pour back in the nihonshu that spilled into the masu.

SHŌCHŪ (24%–45% ABV)

Shōchū
焼酎
shōchū
[sho-oh-choo]

- Nihonshu is made from fermented rice. Shōchū is the distilled version of it, although it can also be made from sweet potatoes, barley, or buckwheat.
- Shōchū can be enjoyed on the rocks or mixed with fruit juice, soda, soda water, or oolong tea—similar to vodka or tequila. Lemon sours made with shōchū are popular among women.

UMESHU (10%–15% ABV)

Umeshu
梅酒
umeshu
[oo-may-shoo]

Alcohol made from plums soaked in shōchū and sugar. The resulting plum wine is very sweet, like a Moscato wine or white port.

HIGHBALL

Highball
ハイボール
highball
[hy-ball]

An extremely popular cocktail consisting of whiskey and soda water over ice. Chūhai [choo-oo-ha-ee] is a version made with shōchū.

SOFT DRINKS

Water and green and oolong teas are available nearly anywhere.

The most common soft drink brands you'll see in Japan are familiar to Westerners: Coca-Cola, Pepsi Cola, Fanta, and Minute Maid. But there are also two other popular sodas that are less commonly seen outside Japan.

Ginger ale
ジンジャーエール
ginger ale
[jin-jah-ah ay-ell-oo]

Homemade Japanese ginger ale can be quite spicy

Melon-flavored soda
メロンソーダ
melon soda
[meh-lon soh-dah]

Credit: DocChewbacca

Ramune
ラムネ
ramune
[lah-moo-nay]

A Japanese lemon-lime soda that comes in a bottle sealed with a marble. To open, find the plunger that comes with the bottle. It will be on top of the cap. Place the plunger on the cap and firmly press down with your palm to dislodge the marble.

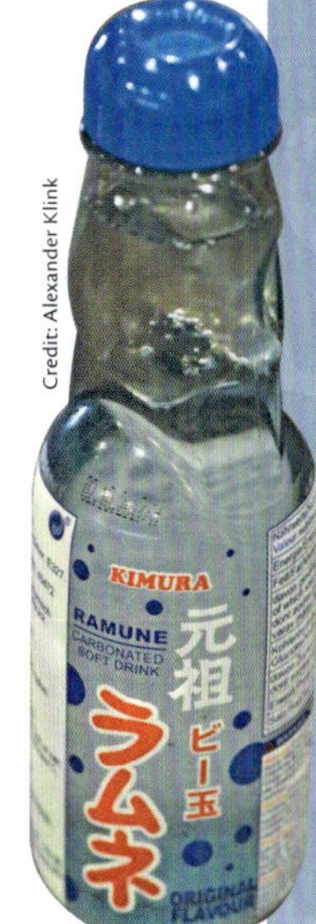

Credit: Alexander Klink

KONBINI

Konbini is the Japanese word for a convenience store, mini-marts that are open 24/7/365. In Tokyo, you'll find them every hundred yards or so.

- The vast majority of konbini are one of three brands: Family Mart, Lawson, or 7-11.
- Three smaller chains are Ministop, Daily Yamazaki, and Sunkus.
- Konbini offer a number of services and sell items such as magazines, emergency products (toiletries, batteries, umbrellas), and most importantly, food and snacks at any time of day or night.
- For the most part, they all sell the same things, with a mix of national and store brands.

Credit: Yuya Tamai

GRAB AND GO

- Salads
- Bento boxes made fresh the same day
- Daily sushi trays
- Heatable meals (omu rice, curry rice, donburi)
- Onigiri, or stuffed rice triangles (おにぎり or お握り)

Common onigiri fillings include:

- Flaked salmon: 紅鮭 / 紅しゃけ (beni shake)
- Tuna salad: ツナマヨネーズ (tsuna mayonezu)
- Salmon roe: イクラ (ikura)
- Pollack roe: 明太子 (mentaiko)
- Pickled plum: 梅 (ume)
- Grilled pork: 焼き豚 (yaki buta)

TIP!

Most onigiri labels include an English translation in the lower left.

NOTE!

Onigiri are cleverly wrapped to keep the seaweed dry and crisp. To unwrap your treat, check out the images on the label.

Pull down on the center strip.

Pull away the plastic on the right half of the onigiri to reveal the seaweed.

Pull away the plastic on the left side to remove it from between the seaweed and rice.

If you've done it correctly, the seaweed should remain intact.

Credit: Marco Verch Professional Photographer and Speaker

Credit: Toshiyuki IMAI

TRIANGLE SANDWICHES

Japanese sandwich bread is so tender that it is used to make sweet sandwiches filled with fruit and whipped cream. These are available next to the savory sandwiches, which generally include ham salad, egg, fried shrimp or pork, and beef.

Credit: Corpse Reviver

SALTY SNACKS

- Chips in various flavors
- Cocktail snacks
- Nuts
- Fish, seafood, and dried seaweed. The most popular are:

Credit: Magnus D

Niboshi
煮干し
Tiny anchovy, also used to make dashi stock

Tazukuri
田作り
Dried candied sardines

BAKERY

- Pastries (croissants, brioches)
- Melon bread: Sweet bread rolls with a crispy top layer with a melon-like design
- Savory treats: Hot dogs, noodle sandwiches

TIP!
The variety of options make konbini a great place to grab breakfast for kids.

COOKIES/CANDY

- Cookies
- Chocolate bars
- Candy

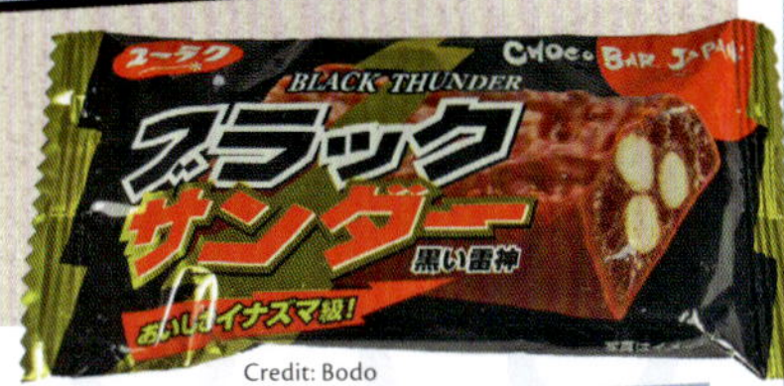

Credit: Bodo

FROZEN FOODS

- Ice cream
- Popsicles

TIP!
Some international brands make flavors sold only in Japan. And not just green tea.

Credit: OpenCage

HOT FOODS AT THE COUNTER

- Fried foods (karaage, korokke, French fries)
- Chuukaman (steamed buns) filled with nikuman (pork) or anman (red bean)

Credit: doronko

Whether or not your konbini has a dining area, the cashier will offer to heat up your meal in a microwave or give you hot water for instant noodles.

Would you like that warmed up?

温めましょうか？
Atatame mashouka?

TIP!
If you don't want your receipt, place it in the container provided for recycling.

TIP!
Some konbini also sell alcohol and/or cigarettes. This will always be advertised on the sign outside: 酒 (alcohol) / たばこ (tobacco).

INSTANT NOODLES

- Instant noodles (ramen, soba, and udon) in a variety of flavors
- Curry noodles

Credit: [puamelia]

SUPERMARKETS

Given the infinite number of ready-to-eat foods available, you might not think to visit a supermarket. But that's where you'll find some hidden gems.

MAJOR CHAINS

Izumi

Aeon

Life

Itō Yōkadō

Uny

Supermarkets get bigger the farther away you get from central Tokyo. Most grocery stores in the city will be small- to medium-size and operate from at least 9 a.m. to 9 p.m.

Unlike Americans, who typically make big grocery store purchases weekly, the Japanese shop for their meals daily. This means that items from meat to fish to prepared meals are replenished daily.

If you're traveling as a group or with your family, buying food at supermarkets instead of konbini can save you quite a bit of money for several reasons.

Konbini prices are higher because they're open around the clock. The same item will cost about 10% less at the supermarket.

Supermarkets carry multiple brands, creating a range of prices for the same product. On the other hand, they don't carry store brands.

Supermarkets carry family-size packages.

Supermarkets regularly hold sales.

Supermarkets carry a much wider variety of hot and cold prepared meals.

TIP!

To reduce waste, prepared meals are discounted starting at 2 p.m. By 7 p.m., discounts can be as much as 50% or even 70% off. You could get a sushi dinner for a song!

The produce section features a wide variety, but fruit can be expensive.

NOTE!

Prices are not per pound but per item or package.

TIP!

Look for slightly damaged or old fruit. They're often discounted.

Credit: Kirakirameister

NOTE!

Because supermarkets are constantly being restocked, you may encounter crates and boxes in the aisle.

Credit: Corpse Reviver

CHECKING OUT

At the register, place your basket in front of the cashier. There is no conveyor belt.

The cashier will scan your items and place them one by one in another basket along with some plastic bags.

TIP!
Bring your own bags to reduce plastic use.
More and more stores are charging for grocery bags to discourage their use.

TIP!
Rolls of plastic bags are available at checkout for fragile items or products likely to drip, along with a machine to seal the bag.

Leave the empty basket at the register.

Pay and take your change.

Take your bags and the basket with your items and move to a separate area to bag your own groceries.

NOTE!
More and more stores are starting to offer self-checkout. Transfer your own items from one basket to another as you scan them. If in doubt, watch the people around you.

TIP!
Supermarkets are the best place to buy souvenir snacks. They're cheaper and the packages are larger.

TIP!
If you need baby food, look in the diaper aisle.

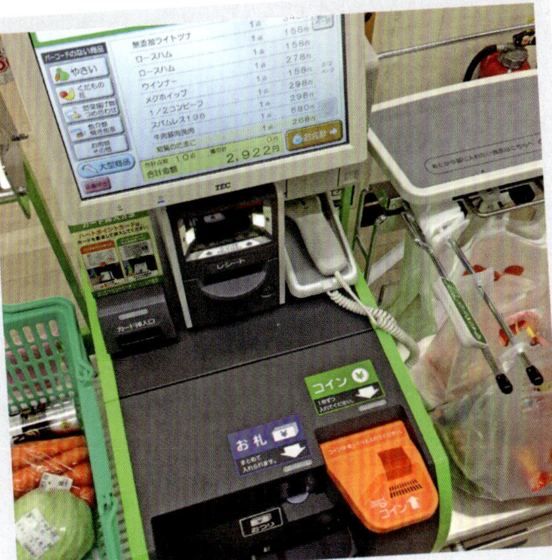

Credit: Karl Baron

VENDING MACHINES

There are 5.5 million vending machines across Japan, or one for every 23 people. They're found nearly everywhere, on every street corner.

Vending machine

自動販売機

jidouhanbaiki
[jee-doh-oh-hahn-by-kee]

jihanki
[jee-hahn-kee]
(for short)

NOTE!

Locals will have an easier time understanding you if you say "bending machines" instead of "vending machines"!

HOW TO USE A VENDING MACHINE

Paying with change

- Insert coins
- Select your item
- Retrieve your item
- Wait a few seconds or press the lever to retrieve your change

Paying with an IC card

- Select your item
- Scan your card on the reader
- Retrieve your item

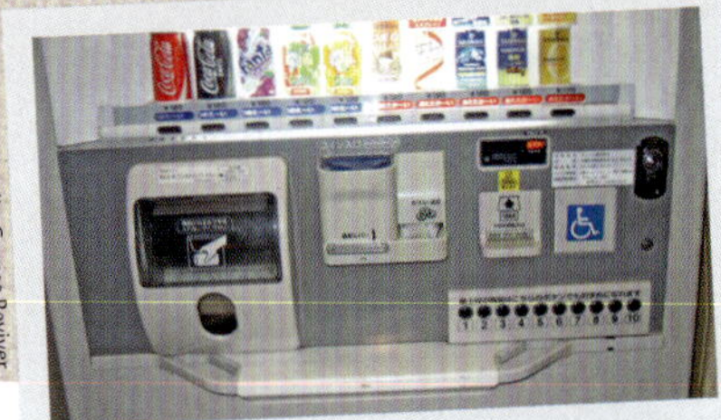

Credit: Corpse Reviver

HOT OR COLD?

Credit: Mj-bird

Cold drinks

- Plain or flavored mineral water.
- Pocari sweat: Supposedly replaces electrolytes lost through sweat . . . and cures hangovers.
- Kirin lemon: Lemon soda, not beer, despite the label and brand.
- Fruit juice: Generally contains only 30% fruit juice concentrate.
- Mets: A Japanese brand of cola.
- Energy drinks: Easily identifiable by their small size.
- Mitsuya cider: Similar to Sprite or 7UP.
- Calpis water: Powdered milk and lactic ferments dissolved in water. Also comes in a carbonated version (Calpis Soda).

Credit: Lordcolus

Cold
つめた〜い

Bottles with blue labels are served cold.

BLUE

Hot
あったか〜い

Bottles with red labels are served hot.

RED

Credit: Pocari Sweat VN

Credit: David Pursehouse

Credit: Immanuel Giel

TIP!

If you like Calpis, you can buy the powdered version at grocery stores and make it at home.

Iced tea
アイスティー

Iced tea
[ice-soo-tee]

TIP!

If you carry a reusable water bottle, you can usually ask to fill it with tap water at any café, konbini, or restaurant.

May I take some water?
水を入れてもいいですか？

Mizu o irete mo ii desuka ?
[mee-zoo ee-ray-tay moh ee-ee day-soo-kah]

TIP!

All vending machines have recycling bins for empty bottles.

Credit: Steve Cadman

NOTE!

Vending machines that sell cigarettes or alcohol require a Taspo card, which is only available to Japanese citizens of legal age. The only place you'll be able to buy alcohol or tobacco is at konbini or supermarkets.

Hot and cold drinks

- **Green tea:** Usually comes in light green bottles.

- **Coffee:** Cans of coffee can be consumed hot or cold. Machines often sell cold coffee in summer, hot coffee in winter.

- **Coffee in cans** is usually sold black with sugar, though some do contain milk. Some are sold without sugar (always called BLACK no matter the brand). Try a few to find your favorite brand!

- **Hot chocolate** ココア (kokoa): May be made with water or milk.

Hot drinks

NOTE!

Hot drinks are generally only available between October and March.

Credit: Kim Unertl

Credit: David Pursehouse

Credit: Christian Kadluba

- **Corn soup**

- **Onion soup**

- **Hot lemon:** Lemon drink excellent for warming up

- **Miso soup**

- **Red bean soup (oshiruko)**

Credit: Jim Epler

EATING ORGANIC/ VEGETARIAN/VEGAN

Japan lags behind other developed countries when it comes to organic food and vegan diets. Still, both have come a long way in recent years.

EATING ORGANIC

The Japanese mostly use the English word to designate organic food: オーガ ニック organic [oh-oh-gah-nee-koo].

Less often, you'll see the Japanese word yuuki 有機 [yoo-oo-kee].

The konbini chain Lawson now has a sister brand called Lawson Natural that carries a wide selection of organic products—although not all items are organic.

Many specialized chain stores have popped up over the past few years. The most popular are:

- Natural House
- Yuuki no Sato 有機の里
- Waseda Natural 早稲田自然食品
- Mothers
- F&F 自然食品の店
- Lima
- Natural Mart

NOTE!
Organic stores are significantly more expensive than conventional supermarkets.

TIP!
Frequented by young women (the main drivers of organic eating in Japan), Omotesandō Avenue has the highest concentration of organic restaurants and stores. There's even a farmers market in front of United Nations University on weekends from 10 a.m. to 4 p.m.

EATING VEGETARIAN/VEGAN

I'm vegetarian
ベジタリアンです

Bejitarian desu
[beh-jee-tar-yan day-soo]

Vegetarian restaurant
ベジタリアンレストラン

Bejitarian resutoran
[beh-jee-tar-yan ray-soo-toh-rahnt]

There are a number of vegetarian and vegan choices at restaurants and izakaya:

- Omelets (not vegan)
- Potato salad (not vegan)
- Vegetable tempura
- Eggplant sushi
- Salad
- Miso eggplant
- Nattō
- Edamame
- Tsukemono
- Daikon radish (ask for shoyu sauce or mirin)
- Sansai (wild mountain vegetables)
- Kinpira (sautéed root vegetables)
- Umeboshi onigiri
- Zaru soba and zaru udon (cold noodles served with dipping sauce; popular in summer)

NOTE!
Make sure to ask whether the broth (dashi) is vegetarian.
Shōjin dashi: 精進出汁

TIP!
Shōjin ryōri 精進料理 [sho-jin ree-oh-oh-lee] is a meat-free, fish-free Buddhist diet. Restaurants will take special care with your meal or will point you to a nearby restaurant that suits your needs.

TOP 3 **VEGAN-FRIENDLY DISHES**

These are the three most common vegan-friendly dishes.
They've been a part of Japanese cuisine for centuries.

3) Mochi 餅

- Mochi: A sticky rice paste used in soups, desserts, crackers, and more.
- Dango mochi 団子餅: A skewer of three mochi balls.
- Daifuku 大福: Stuffed mochi balls, usually filled with red bean paste or fruit.
- Arare 霰: Savory mochi crackers that are dried and toasted.
- Agemochi 揚げ餅: Fried mochi snacks.

2) Tofu 豆腐

- Tofu is essentially soy milk cheese. It can be served a variety of ways, including in soups and salads. The three most common types are:
- Kinugoshidōfu 絹ごし豆腐: Silken
- Momendōfu 木綿豆腐: Firm
- Agedashidōfu 揚げ出し豆腐: Fried

1) Rice 御飯 (gohan)

You'll find white rice everywhere, even drizzled with green tea at the end of a meal (ochazuke).

Credit: Alice Wiegand

RAMEN

Credit: hiroshikato

Some restaurants offer vegetarian or even vegan ramen bowls. The most famous is Ramen Ouka in Shinjuku.

TIP!
The HappyCow app lists nearby vegan restaurants. The Halal Gourmet Japan app is also handy (see next page).

AT THE **KONBINI**

I'm vegan
ビーガンです

Biigan desu
[bee-ee-gahn day-soo]

Vegan restaurant
ビーガンレストラン

Biigan resutoran
[bee-ee-gahn ray-soo-toh-rahnt]

TIP!
Fast-food chains, including CoCo Curry and MOS Burger, are starting to offer vegetarian options.

If you buy a salad, make sure the dressing is on the side. It will be labeled ドレッシング 別売り dressing betsuuri.

NOTE!
SOYJOY bars are not necessarily vegan. They can contain dairy or honey.

TIP!
In Japan, most jiggly desserts are made of agar-agar, not gelatin.
Jelly dessert: ゼリー zerii
[zell-ee-ee]

Soy milk (tōny 豆乳 [toh-oh-nee-yoo-oo]) and almond milk (almond milk アーモンドミルク [ah-ah-mond-oh mee-loo-koo]) are widely available.

Does this contain animal products?

動物製品が入って
いますか？

Dōbutsu seihin
ga haitteimasu ka?
[doh-oh-boo-tsoo say-heen gah
ha-ee-Ø-tay-mahss-kah]

EATING **HALAL/KOSHER**

Though they represent a tiny portion of Tokyo's 150,000 restaurants, you should be able to find certified halal and kosher restaurants fairly easily.

TIP!

Much of the info in the two previous pages applies to halal and kosher diets as well.

NOTE!

If your diet doesn't allow for vinegar, watch out for sushi rice, which contains rice vinegar. Order sashimi instead with a side of white rice.

RAMEN

Most ramen is not halal. In addition to the pork slices it's served with, the broth is simmered with pork bones. Some restaurants offer 100% halal chicken, the most famous being Honolu Ebisu (Ebisu district) and Ramen Ouka (Shinjuku district).

RESTAURANTS AND **KEBAB HOUSES**

Credit: shankar s.

Since many Japanese find the flavor of lamb overwhelming, gyros are usually made with beef and/or chicken.

As with all Tokyo restaurants, quality can vary widely. Look for establishments with long lines.

AT THE SUPERMARKET/**KONBINI**

If you're unsure about a product (freeze-dried noodles, flavored chips), look for the following kanji characters in the ingredient list:

Pork
豚
buta
[boo-tah]

Pig meat
豚肉
butaniku
[boo-tah-nee-koo]

If necessary, you can tell an employee:

I don't eat pork
豚肉はだめです
Buta niku wa dame desu
[boo-tah nee-koo wah dah-may day-soo]

TIP!

The area around the Tokyo mosque 東京ジャーミイ (Tokyo Camii) is teeming with halal eateries. Go for prayers early on in your trip and talk to locals, who will have the best recommendations for Tokyo restaurants. The mosque's hours are available at http://tokyocamii.org.

TIP!

The Halal Gourmet Japan app lists halal restaurants and grocery stores. You can even snap a photo of a store shelf and the app will indicate which products are "Muslim-friendly" and list their ingredients.

Credit: Wiiii

KEY WORDS AND **PHRASES**

AT THE **HOSTESS STAND**

Number of people
1 Ichimei [eet-shee-may]
2 Nimei [nee-may]
3 Sanmei [sahn-may]
4 Yonmei [yon-may]
5 Gomei [go-may]
6 Rokumei [rock-oo-may]
7 Nanamei [nah-nah-may]
8 Hachimei [aht-shee-may]
9 Kyuumei [kee-oo-oo-may]
10 Juumei [joo-oo-may]

Smoking
喫煙席
kitsuenseki
[kee-tsoo-en-say-kee]

Nonsmoking
禁煙席
kinenseki
[kee-nen-say-kee]

PREPARING **TO ORDER**

I'd like to order
注文をお願いします
Chūmon wo onegaishimasu
[choo-oo-mon oh oh-nay-gah-ee-shee-mass]

What do you recommend?
お勧めは？
Osusume wa ?
[oh-soo-soo-may wah]

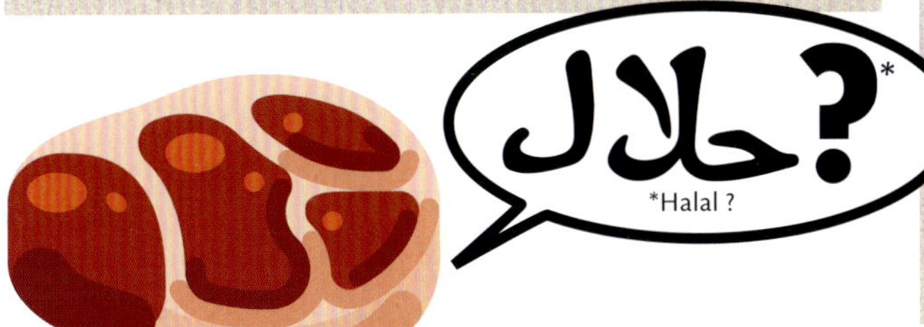

ASKING FOR A **MENU**

Do you have a menu in French?
フランス語のメニューがありますか？
Furansugo no menyuu ga arimasuka ?
[foo-lahn-soo-go no may-nee-oo gah ah-ree-mahss-kah]

Do you have a menu in English?
英語のメニューがありますか？
Eigo no menyuu ga arimasuka ?
[ay-go no may-nee-oo gah ah-ree-mahss-kah]

Do you have a children's menu?
お子様メニューがありますか？
Okosama menyuu ga arimasu ka?
[oh-koh-sah-mah may-nee-oo gah ah-lee-mahss-kah]

Do you have a vegetarian menu?
ベジタリアンメニューがありますか？
Bejitarian menyuu ga arimasu ka?
[beh-jee-tah-ree-ahn may-nee-oo gah ah-lee-mahss-kah]

Do you have a vegan menu?
ビーガンメニューがありますか？
Biigan menyuu ga arimasu ka?
[bee-ee-gahn may-nee-oo gah ah-lee-mahss-kah]

Do you have a halal menu?
ハラールメニューがありますか？
Harāru menyuu ga arimasu ka?
[hah-lah-ah-loo may-nee-oo gah ah-lee-mahss-kah]

SPECIAL DIETS/ALLERGIES/INTOLERANCES

I can't eat meat
お肉は食べられません
Oniku wa taberaremasen
[oh-nee-koo wah tah-bay-lah-lay-mah-sen]

I'm allergic to ___.
___アレルギーがあります。
___arerugii ga arimasu.
[___ ah-lay-roo-ghee-ee gah ah-lee-mahss]

Hold the ___, please
___なしでお願いします
___nashi de onegaishimasu
[___ nah-shee day oh-nay-gah-ee-shee-mahss]

Is it spicy?
辛いですか？
Karai desuka ?
[kah-lye day-soo-kah]

ORDERING

This one, please	I'd like the same thing (as your neighbor)	Another one, please	That's it (for now)
これをください	同じものをください	お代わりください	(取り敢えず) 以上 で
Kore wo kudasai	Onajimono wo kudasai	Okawari kudasai	(Toriaezu) ijō de
[koh-lay oh koo-dah-sy]	[oh-nah-jee-mo-no koo-dah-sy]	[oh-kah-wah-ree koo-dah-sy]	[(toh-ree-ah-ay-zoo) ee-jo-oh day]

ASKING FOR **THE CHECK**

Check, please

お会計をお願いします

Okaikei wo onegaishimasu
[oh-ky-kay-ee wo oh-nay-gah-ee-shee-mahss]

MEALS

Breakfast	Lunch	Dinner
朝御飯 or 朝ご飯	昼御飯 or 昼ご飯	晩御飯 or 晩ご飯
asagohan	hirugohan	bangohan
[ah-sah-go-hahn]	[hee-loo-go-hahn]	[bahn-go-hahn]

STAPLES

Cooked rice	Soy sauce	Stock/broth	Miso	Miso soup
御飯 or ご飯	醤油	出汁	みそ or 味噌	みそ汁 or 味噌汁
gohan	shōyu	dashi	miso	misoshiru
[go-hahn]	[sho-oh-yoo]	[dah-shee]	[mee-soh]	[mee-soh-shee-roo]

WATER **AND TEA**

Water	Tea	Green tea	Matcha tea	Barley tea	Black tea	Oolong tea
水	お茶	煎茶	抹茶	麦茶	紅茶	烏龍茶
mizu	ocha	sencha	matcha	mugicha	koocha	ūroncha
[mee-zoo]	[oh-cha]	[sen-cha]	[mah-cha]	[moo-ghee-cha]	[koh-oh-cha]	[oh-oh-lohn-cha]

SILVERWARE

Napkin	Chopsticks	Knife	Fork	Spoon
お絞り	箸	ナイフ	フォーク	スプーン
oshibori	hashi	knife	fork	spoon
[oh-shee-bo-ree]	[ha-shee]	[nah-ee-foo]	[fo-oh-koo]	[soo-poo-oon]

SUSHI

Sushi	Sashimi	Pickled ginger
寿司	刺身	ガリ
		gari
		[gah-lee]
Chirashi	Wasabi	
散らし	山葵	

NOODLES

Ramen
ラーメン or らーめん

Shio Ramen	Shōyu Ramen
塩ラーメン	醤油ラーメン
Miso Ramen	**Tonkotsu Ramen**
味噌ラーメン	豚骨ラーメン

Small size	Medium size	Large size
並盛り	中盛り	大盛り
namimori	chuumori	oomori

Udon	Soba
うどん or 饂飩	そば or 蕎麦

DONBURI

Rice bowl topped with:

Sliced beef	Breaded pork cutlet
牛丼	カツ丼
gyūdon	katsudon
[ghee-oo-oo-don]	[kat-soo-don]
Tempura	**Egg and chicken**
天丼	親子丼
tendon	oyakodon
[ten-don]	[oh-yah-koh-don]

POPULAR DISHES

Curry rice	Tempura	Yakiniku	Shabu-shabu	Sukiyaki
カレーライス	天麩羅	焼肉	しゃぶしゃぶ	すき焼き or 鋤焼
karē rice	tempura	yakiniku	shabu-shabu	sukiyaki
[kah-lay ry-soo]	[ten-poo-rah]	[yah-kee-nee-koo]	[shah-boo shah-boo]	[soo-kee-yah-kee]

Karaage	Korokke	Tori karaage	Takoyaki
唐揚げ	コロッケ	とり唐揚げ	たこ焼き
karaage	korokke	tori karaage	takoyaki
[kah-rah-ah-gay]	[koh-lohk-kay]	[toh-lee kah-rah-ah-gay]	[tah-koh-yah-kee]

Breaded pork cutlet	Omu rice	Yakitori
豚カツ	オムライス	焼鳥
tonkatsu	omu rice	yakitori
[ton-kah-tsoo]	[oh-moo ry-soo]	[yah-kee-toh-ree]

Yakitori condiments

Salt	Sweet sauce
塩	垂れ
shio	tare
[shee-oh]	[tah-ray]

ALL YOU CAN **EAT/DRINK**

All you can eat
食べ放題

tabehōdai
[tah-bay-ho-oh-dye]

All you can drink
飲み放題

nomihōdai
[no-mee-ho-oh-dye]

VEGETARIAN/VEGAN

Does this contain animal product?
動物製品が入っていますか ？

Dōbutsu seihin ga haitteimasu ka?
[doh-oh-boo-tsoo say-heen gah ha-ee-Ø-tay-mahss-kah]

Mochi
餅

mochi
[moh-chee]

Tofu
豆腐

tōfu
[toh-foo]

Soy milk
豆乳

tōnyū
[toh-oh-nee-yoo-oo]

Almond milk
アーモンドミルク

almond milk
[ah-ah-mon-doh mee-loo-koo]

Jell-O
ゼリー

zerii
[zeh-lee-ee]

HALAL

Pork
豚

buta
[boo-tah]

Pig meat
豚肉

butaniku
[boo-tah-nee-koo]

I don't eat pork
豚肉はだめです

Buta niku wa dame desu
[boo-tah nee-koo wah dah-may day-soo]

AT THE **BAR**

Who wants to drink ___?
…飲む人？

... nomu hito ?
[____ no-moo hee-toh]

The same thing (to drink)
もう一杯同じ物ください

Mō ippai onaji mono kudasai
[moh-oh ee-Ø-py oh-nah-jee mo-no koo-dah-sy]

Alcohol
酒 or お酒

sake or osake
[sah-kay] or [oh-sah-kay]

Beer
ビール

bīru
[bee-ee-loo]

Happōshu
発泡酒

happōshu
[hap-poh-shoo]

Nihonshu
日本酒

nihonshu
[nee-hon-shoo]

Shōchū
焼酎

shōchū
[sho-choo]

Umeshu
梅酒

umeshu
[oo-may-shoo]

Highball
ハイボール

highball
[hy-ball]

Chūhai
チューハイ

chūhai
[choo-hy]

Melon soda
メロンソーダ

Ginger ale
ジンジャーエール

Ramune
ラムネ

TO GO

Onigiri
おにぎり or お握り

onigiri
[oh-nee-ghee-lee]

Lunch set
弁当

bentō
[ben-toh-oh]

THINGS TO DO

ARCADES

An integral part of Japanese life for forty years, arcades have evolved over time but are still enjoyed by the young and the young at heart.

NOTE!

Arcade machines only accept ¥100 coins. Bring a handful with you or make change at a machine.

Coins

硬貨

kōka
[koh-oh-kah]

Change machine

両替機

ryōgae-ki
[ree-oh-oh-gah-ay-kee]

THERE ARE TWO TYPES OF ARCADES IN JAPAN

Specialized arcades

Many arcades feature a theme, from retro games to racing games, shooting games to one-on-one games, analog games and more. Each one is tailored to a certain type of video game–lover, so find an arcade that speaks to you. They're also fun to wander around in for the ambience and to watch some seriously impressive game play.

Generalist arcades

Generalist arcades offer a wide variety of games and are more approachable for the average player, though you'll still find avid gamers looking to play the latest releases.

Generalist arcades are usually owned by video game companies (Namco, Sega, Taito). Each floor has its own theme, with themes varying from district to district. The most popular themes are shown below.

CLAW MACHINES

Claw machines are always on the first floor and sometimes overflow onto another floor. They're easy for even young kids to grasp and are rarely rigged. That means with a bit of skill you could leave with an armful of prizes.

TIP!

If you've been working on the same machine for a while with no success, speak to an employee. They'll give you tips or even move the item to a better position.

TYPES OF GAMES

Music/Rhythm

These may seem easy, but they require lightning-fast reflexes. Watch the more experienced players before attempting it yourself.

Shooting/Fighting/Driving

These games are the most intuitive, but if you go up against a local, watch out!

Online

Some games let you play against opponents in other arcades around the country. There are even entire floors dedicated to online gaming.

Kids

Many arcade machines spit out collectible cards. A card costs a hundred yen, and you can win more by winning fights or challenges.

Virtual reality

Usually the most expensive games.

TIP!

Headphone jacks are always provided for music and rhythm games.

NOTE!

Online games require a membership card. Ask an employee for help.

NOTE!

Virtual reality games are played online and usually require a membership card.

PURIKURA

Purikura
プリクラ

purikura
[poo-lee-koo-lah]

Purikura is a shortening of the Japanese pronunciation of "print club."

The purikura floor is the easiest to spot, as it is generally only frequented by women and girls, occasionally accompanied by a boyfriend. Men who enter in groups receive stares. Men entering alone are viewed with suspicion.

NOTE!

Some establishments specializing in purikura, including Harajuku, prohibit men from entering unless accompanied by a woman.

Purikura are photo booths offering seemingly infinite ways to edit and decorate photos to make them as cute as possible. The activity is usually done as a group, but you can take a solo photo and create your own unique, personalized souvenir.

Credit: hildgrim

Credit: Dick Thomas Johnson_

THE PHOTOSHOOT

Before

- A generously equipped space is provided for you to do your makeup.
- Select a photo booth and pay the fee (generally ¥400).
- Choose your settings: full-body or portrait, background color, filters, poses, etc.
- Enter your email address where the photos should be sent.
- Go inside the photo booth and stow your belongings in the area provided.

During

- Position your feet as instructed. This will vary based on the photo size and may change throughout the session.
- Copy the suggested poses or create your own.
- Each session results in five to six photos.

AFTER THE PHOTOSHOOT

Retro

Lower levels are usually dedicated to games that are older but still popular. These areas are most often frequented by older men and generally allow smoking, causing them to smell like stale cigarette smoke.

TIP!

Some arcades feature floors dedicated entirely to analog games (pool, darts, bowling).

Credit: Ominae

Customize your photo by applying filters, adding icons and text, or enlarging your eyes. Edits are made using a stylus, and options vary from machine to machine. The only limit is how much time you have!

TIP!

For your first purikura, choose one of the less busy photo booths. The timers give you more time to peruse your options. The more popular machines give you less time to decide.

Select the photo sizes, then confirm your selection. If the machine didn't ask for your email address earlier, enter it now.

Exit the photo booth and wait about a minute. The machine will spit out your purikura. Scissors may be provided so you can share the photos among your group.

KARAOKE

Karaoke in Japan is nothing like karaoke in the USA! In Japan, karaoke is enjoyed in a private room among a small group of friends.

RENTING A **KARAOKE ROOM**

- Find a business with a sign that says カラオケ (karaoke).

- Fill out the form at the front desk. The next time you come back, you'll only have to give your name.

- Indicate how many people are in your group and how long you wish to stay.

- You may be asked which provider you prefer, DAM or JoySound. Choose DAM if you can, since it has features useful to tourists.

- You are generally expected to purchase drinks. Choose from the menu. Most establishments offer nomihōdai (all you can drink) options, alcoholic beverages, and soft drinks (fountain drinks upstairs).

- You'll be handed a ticket with a room number. Keep it and go to the floor where your room is located.

NOTE!
Some karaoke bars offer extras at the front desk, such as costumes or headsets. Ask for the price. Sometimes they're free!

Once you've selected your song, you can change the key using the Key Control option. Press + to modulate upward or − to modulate downward. Hit Send to send the song to the queue.

TIP!
You can adjust the key or tempo in the middle of the song directly on the machine.

Credit: Dick Thomas Johnson

While one person is singing, the next people in line can select their songs. Each room has two microphones, so you can even sing duets.

IN THE **ROOM**

On the tablet provided, select multilingual mode.

For songs in English

Choose English. You can search for songs by title or artist. Select the one you want and press Request/Send, the red button in the lower right.

For songs in Japanese

In DAM

- In the language selection menu, you'll see two other options on the right:

- "Japanese Songs" (Romanized Japanese): The most popular songs with subtitles on the screen in the Roman alphabet.

- "Watch Lyrics" (Romanized Japanese): Lyrics appear on the tablet in the Roman alphabet alongside the Japanese. Works with any song but requires use of the tablet.

In JoySound

- In the English menu, you'll find the most popular Japanese songs with subtitles on the screen in the Roman alphabet.

- You can use the "Watch Lyrics" feature with any song, but only on the tablet.

NOTE!
Not all options may be available, depending on the software version you're using. You can always look up lyrics in romaji on your phone.

TIP!
If you go into Japanese mode on the machine, you'll need to use the kana alphabet (see appendices). Look for the かな (kana) and 英数 (eisu) buttons. Press the latter to switch to the Roman alphabet.

NOTE!

If you're with Japanese people, note that the custom is for everyone to sing when it's their turn. You can also jump in and sing backup or play the maracas or tambourine!

You can order food or drinks at any time from the menu on the table. Just pick up the phone and order. Your food will be brought to the room shortly.

The phone will ring ten minutes before the end of your time slot. Pay the bill and wrap things up.

At the front desk, it's customary to split the bill equally, since everyone used the room.

Function	Lyrics
機能	歌詞
kinou	kashi
[kee-noo]	[kah-shee]

Song	Singer
曲	歌手
kyokyu	kashu
[kee-oh-kee-oo]	[kah-shoo]

Song title	Artist
曲名	歌手名
kyokyumei	kashumei
[kee-oh-kee-oo-may]	[kah-shoo-may]

COST

The cost of karaoke varies depending on the bar, the district, whether you have a membership card, and especially the time of day and day of the week.

Prices are given for increments of thirty minutes, but unlimited ("Free Time") options are also available. The cost varies depending on the time period.

TIP!

Depending on your reserved time, you may be able to ask for another hour. You'll be billed accordingly.

TIP!

A nearby karaoke bar is a great backup plan for entertainment during inclement weather.

Credit: Rog01

WHAT **TO SING**

Catalogs of English songs include thousands of hits from the 1960s to today.

Credit: booby bubio

PET CAFÉS

Tokyoites spend most of their day working, so most don't have time to care for a pet. Pet cafés are a way to fill the gap.

WHAT IS A **PET CAFÉ?**

A pet café is a place to enjoy a beverage while interacting with animals. They began with cats in Osaka in 2004 and grew in popularity. Now you can find pet cafés featuring all kinds of animals, including:

- Cats
- Dogs
- Rabbits
- Parakeets
- Ferrets
- Hedgehogs
- Owls
- Reptiles
- Miniature pigs
- Otters

Credit: Philippe Vallotti

Credit: Takashi Hososhima

COST

- Pet cafés charge for:
- The duration of your session, in ten-minute increments
- A one-drink minimum

Credit: calamity_sal

PET CAFÉ **RULES AND ETIQUETTE**

Rules vary from café to café but will be made explicit before you enter. However, you'll encounter the following every time:

- You'll need to take off your shoes and put on the slippers provided.
- Entryways are enclosed to prevent animals from escaping.
- Make sure to disinfect your hands before entering.
- For sanitary reasons, food and drinks must be consumed in a separate room from the animals.

- Do not disturb sleeping animals. Avoid making too much noise.
- Take as many selfies as you want but DO NOT USE FLASH!
- You can purchase treats to hand out, but make sure to spread the love to all the animals.
- Wash your hands before you leave. After all, dozens of customers have handled those cats! If the animals are furry (dogs, cats), brushes are available to clean off your clothes.

Credit: John Gillespie

ANIMAL WELFARE

NOTE!

With the rise in popularity of pet cafés, there will inevitably be some with shady practices. Many pet cafés have been forced to shut down after inspection. Although oversight has become stricter and more frequent, nasty surprises are still possible, especially in cafés with wild animals (owls, otters).

TIP!

If you want to be absolutely sure of the animals' welfare, visit a Neco Republic café. Each of the chain's stores is home to stray cats that are all adoptable.

TIP!

You can also rent a dog from the Dog Heart dog café near Yoyogi Park and take them for a walk.
http://dog-heart.ico.bz/index.html

Credit: Philippe Vallotti

ZOOS AND AQUARIUMS

Edogawa Natural Zoo

Located west of Tokyo, Edogawa Natural Zoo is more of an outdoor animal reserve focused on teaching conservation. There are plenty of opportunities for interaction, especially for young kids, including feeding times, a stockyard of animals, and pony rides.

Stations: Nishi-Kasai (T-16) or Funabori (S-17)

Ueno Zoo (恩賜上野動物園)

Established in 1882 and situated within Ueno Park, the zoo is home to 3,000 animals of 500 different species, including two pandas, a local favorite.

NOTE!

At a mere 35 acres, Ueno Zoo feels somewhat cramped.

Station: Ueno (see p. 30)

Sumida Aquarium

As an archipelago, Japan has a close relationship with marine life. Sumida Aquarium is located at the foot of the Tokyo Skytree tower and is the most modern of the country's many aquariums. The tanks are built to accommodate the (modest) size of each species.

Station: Oshiage (A-20, Z-14, KS-45, TS-03)

Maxwell Aqua Park Shinagawa

This marine park is best known for its dolphin show, but it's also home to giant manta rays that you can view from inside an underwater tunnel. Located within a hotel complex, it includes a carousel, a pirate ship, and a bar with tables made of jellyfish tanks.

Station: Shinagawa (see p. 31)

Credit: Zengame

GIFTS FOR YOUR PET

Worried that your pet is missing you back home? Bring them a souvenir! Japanese pet shops offer endless outfits, accessories, and toys for your furry friend.

Toy	Dog toy	Cat toy
おもちゃ	犬のおもちゃ	猫のおもちゃ
omocha	inu no omocha	neko no omocha
[oh-moh-cha]	[ee-noo no oh-mo-cha]	[nay-koh no oh-mo-cha]

100-YEN SHOPS

With their affordable prices, 100-yen shops are the perfect place for locals to grab daily necessities—and for tourists to pick up souvenirs.

As the name suggests, 100-yen shops are stores where everything costs ¥100.

100-yen shop

百円ショップ

hyaku-en shoppu
[hee-ah-koo en shop-poo]

100-yen

百均

hyakkin
[hee-yahk-keen]

NOTE!
Prices do not include tax. The final price is ¥110 per item, or about $0.75.

NOTE!
Some items cost more (¥200 to ¥500). They will be labeled with the price.

The most popular chains are:

Daiso, pioneer and market leader

Can Do

Seria

Daikoku

Flets

Lawson Store 100 is a konbini whose products are packaged to cost ¥100 each.

Credit: Nandaro

Credit: Solomon2C

The thousands of items for sale can be loosely grouped into three categories:

Items for daily use	Souvenir gifts	Hobby supplies and time- and money-savers

Here are some ideas for souvenirs to bring back home, chosen for their small size and weight—two important factors when it comes time to repack your suitcase.

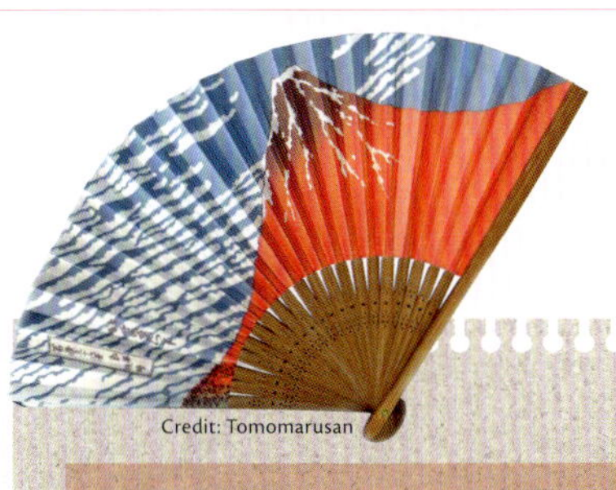

Credit: Tomomarusan

DISHWARE

Travel silverware, if you prefer them over chopsticks

Traditional cups, bowls, saucers, decorative chopsticks and chopstick holders

If you have young children, make sure to hit the aisle with plastic kawaii dishware

TECH/ELECTRONICS

110V/USB adapters, USB cables

Decorative smartphone cases. NOTE! Most are made for iPhones.

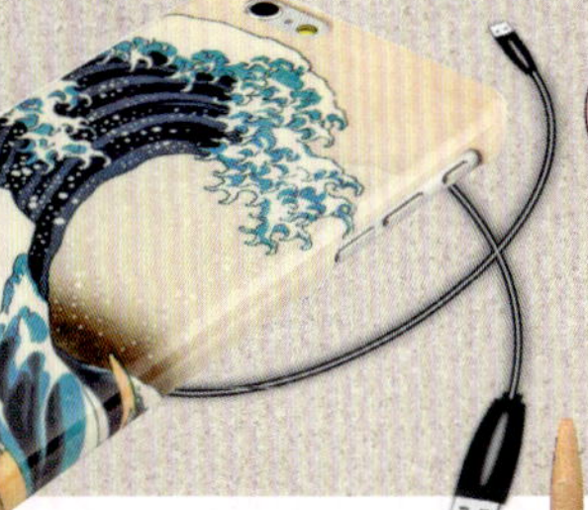

TIP!

Many of the decorative lights sold run on alkaline or mercury batteries. Make sure to stock up while you're there!

NOTE!

Alkaline batteries sold at 100-yen shops may last just as long as (or even longer than) batteries sold at regular stores, or they might die within a couple of hours. Buy the store brand if possible. Otherwise, buy packs of batteries in multiple brands to spread the risk.

Credit: Tomomarusan

TOYS

Traditional cup and ball toy

けん玉

kendama
[ken-dahm-ah]

- Carnival masks
- Licensed toys
- Bubble wands

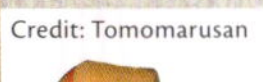

Credit: Akiyoshi's Room

KITCHEN

At 100-yen shops, you'll find endless accessories for the kitchen and table. Regardless of your cooking skills, invest in these Japanese household favorites:

Plastic wrap: The Japanese kind unrolls cleanly.

Stainless steel soap, which removes odors from your hands.

STATIONERY

The Japanese are meticulous about handwriting, making the stationery aisle a treasure trove!

- Coloring books for kids and adults
- Sushi-shaped erasers
- Pencils
- Origami paper
- Calligraphy brushes and paper

- If you have kids, now is the time to get a deal on school supplies!
- You can also stock up on markers and colored pencils for home.

Credit: Laitche

TOILETRIES AND COSMETICS

Credit: Zephyris

Face Towel
フェイスタオル

feisu toalu
[fay-ee-soo toh-ah-loo]

- A microfiber towel, essential in summertime
- Toiletries you may have forgotten at home: combs, tweezers, makeup remover wipes

If you like fake lashes and nails, you'll love a 100-yen shop!

> ### NOTE!
> Skip the makeup (foundation, lipstick) and toothbrushes.

Credit: Crisco 1492

HARDWARE

- Measuring tapes
- Allen wrenches (hex keys)
- Japanese paintbrushes with angled handles

NOTIONS

- Balls of yarn
- Knitting accessories

GARDENING

- Seed packets for flowers and vegetables

Credit: Marco Verch Professional Photographer and Speaker

Credit: DeepSkyBlue

Credit: Tsuda

STORAGE AND TRAVEL

Vacuum-sealed bags help save space in your luggage for the return home.

Credit: Christine Warner

> ### NOTE!
> Avoid storage items with suction cups. They usually don't last long.

THREE MORE SOUVENIR SHOPS

A discussion on souvenir shops wouldn't be complete without these three chains with dozens of locations around Tokyo. There, you'll find unique gifts in every price range. And if you spend more than ¥5,000, you get a tax exemption.

Don Quijote （ドン・キホーテ）

Although the store (pronounced [don kee-roh-tay] is named after the classic literary character, its mascot is a blue penguin. The store carries everything from socks to pressure cookers to suitcases. Don't bring too much with you into the store, as the aisles are cramped and narrow, and a bulky backpack is a disaster waiting to happen. The shop attracts tourists and locals alike, the latter of whom come for the eccentric costumes in the gag gift aisle, the silly gadgets, and the pastries. The Japanese often shorten the name to Donki [don-kee].

FOOD AND DRINK

The drinks are the same as you'll find in any vending machine, but ¥20 or ¥30 cheaper.

- Sweet and salty snacks, candy in unique flavors
- Matcha tea

NOTE!

You'll see numerous licensed products (Hello Kitty, Gudetama, Pokémon, Disney), which vary based on the chain and its partnerships.

NOTE!

This is only a glimpse of the items you'll find. There are plenty of other surprises, including limited-time seasonal items for Christmas, Halloween, spring (cherry blossom products), and summer (fireworks).

TIP!

Some items are sold in multiples. For example, for a total of ¥110, you can buy two seed packets for your garden or three lollipops. You can mix and match the varieties as long as you arrive at the register with the correct number.

CHECKING OUT

- Just like at the supermarket, place your basket at the cash register counter.
- The cashier will count the number of items and transfer them to an empty basket. If you've selected a more expensive item, the cashier will draw your attention to the price to confirm.
- Once you've paid, take the basket with your items and the plastic bags provided to the counter by the door. Old newspapers are available to wrap fragile items.

Credit: Marco Verch Professional Photographer and Speaker

TIP!

There are also 300-yen shop chains (¥330 with sales tax) that carry fewer goods but are still an ideal place to find inexpensive souvenirs. The best-known companies are:

3 Coins

Oho!Ho!

Smart Life Market

Coucou

Tokyu Hands

Tokyu Hands shops also sell an enormous range of items, but they're less kitschy than at Don Quijote. The merchandise tends to be sleeker and more elegant. The aisles are wider, and the stationery and kitchen sections feature some truly marvelous designs. It's well worth a visit. And with its large selection of craft supplies, Tokyu Hands is a must for hobbyists and makers.

Village Vanguard

Billing itself as an "exciting bookstore," Village Vanguard is *the* place for on-trend merchandise and accessories. A favorite shopping spot for hipsters, the chain has numerous partnerships with major pop culture companies, resulting in a huge selection of licensed products. It's a great place for unique souvenirs for lovers of manga and video games.

Credit: Sungdo Cho

TOKYO IN **SPRING**

	March 1–15	March 16–31	April 1–15	April 16–30	May 1–15	May 16–31
Average temperature	40°F–60°F	45°F–63°F	45°F–66°F	54°F–68°F	57°F–73°F	57°F–79°F
Weather	☀	☀	☀	☀	☀	🌧

NOTE!

If you're allergic to pollen, you may want to avoid the period from early March to mid-April.

DRESSING FOR THE WEATHER

Early March

The tail end of winter, but usually still chilly. Bring a heavy coat or fleece jacket. Indoor temperatures vary widely, so wear layers. Bring tights if you plan to wear skirts or dresses.

Mid-March to mid-May

The mild weather in late March brings an explosion of cherry blossoms. Pack a light jacket that's easy to carry around on warm afternoons. Wear layers, such as a sweater or long-sleeved shirt over a T-shirt.

Late May

Bring light, waterproof clothing. The rainy season starts toward the end of the month.

WHAT TO DO/SEE IN SPRING

Hanami
(late March to mid-April)

Hanami ("viewing the flowers") consists of picnicking under flowering cherry trees. If you want to partake in this tradition, you'll want to bring a tarp, which you can buy at the nearest konbini.

Spread out the tarp in an empty spot in the park, take off your shoes, and enjoy your picnic!

When you're done, toss your waste into one of the giant trash cans nearby.

If you can't find a spot to spread out, buy food from a food stall and enjoy it while strolling around the park.

Tarp
(comes from the English term *leisure suit***)**

レジャーシート

lejāshito
[lay-jah-ah-shee-ee-toh]

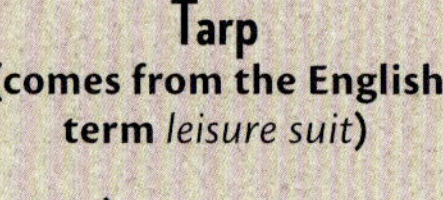

Credit: 江戸村のとくぞう

Hina Matsuri
(March 3)

Doll's Day or Girls' Day, when dolls representing members of the imperial court are put on display.

Kodomo no hi
(May 5)

On Children's Day, families fly banners in the shape of carp fish.

Kanda Matsuri
(around May 15)

The larger version of the festival takes place in Tokyo in odd-numbered years and features a giant parade. The festival is smaller in even-numbered years.

Sanja Matsuri
(third weekend of May)

This traditional festival draws nearly two million people to the Sensō-ji temple area in the Asakusa district.

TOKYO IN **SUMMER**

	June 1–15	June 16–30	July 1–15	July 16–31	August 1–15	August 16–31
Average temperature	64°F–79°F	68°F–81°F	68°F–86°F	70°F–88°F	72°F–95°F	72°F–95°F
Weather						

WHAT TO DO/SEE IN SUMMER

Sanno Matsuri (around June 16)
This festival is only held in even-numbered years, with a giant parade in Chiyoda ward.

Clothing sales (early July)

Mt. Fuji climbing season runs from July to August

Tanabata Festival (July 7)
The Star Festival marking the start of summer. There are fun activities during the day and also at night.

Obon [oh-bon] (August 13–15)
This celebration of ancestral spirits includes a bon-odori [bon-oh-doh-lee], a dance circle around a scaffold. Anyone can join in! The dance steps are simple and easy to learn.

Fireworks
Public fireworks displays are frequent in summer. Here are some tips to make the event more enjoyable:

Arrive several hours in advance.

Purchase a tarp from a nearby konbini (see p. 84) and find an empty spot to spread it out. Remove your shoes and have a seat.

Make sure to take your tarp and trash with you when you leave.

NOTE!
Sunscreen is essential in July and August. Wear SPF 50 if you're sensitive to the sun.

Credit: Kenneth Lu

DRESSING FOR THE WEATHER

June
Tsuyu [tsoo-yoo], the rainy season, lasts for about three weeks in June, when the weather alternates between sunny skies, hours-long torrential downpours, and brief showers. Wear short-sleeved shirts, dresses, and light pants in a quick-drying fabric. And make sure to bring a windbreaker or poncho.

July–August
Summer weather can be sticky, with temperatures in the upper eighties and humidity of 70 to 80%. You'll want to wear T-shirts, tank tops, shorts, capri pants, or skirts. And bring a cap, hat, or parasol for the sun.

NOTE!
Wear socks, even with sandals or ballet flats. You never know when you'll need to take off your shoes. As a rule, the Japanese generally only go barefoot at home.

TIP!
In Japan, you can buy scarf-like towels that are a real life-saver. Wear it around your neck to:
Protect against the sun
Wipe away sweat
Wear as a scarf in drafty places

TIP!
Major apparel brands, including Airism by Uniqlo, make clothing specially designed for humid weather.

TOKYO IN **FALL**

	Sept. 1–15	Sept. 16–30	Oct. 1–15	Oct. 16–31	Nov. 1–15	Nov. 16–30
Average temperature	68°F–86°F	64°F–79°F	59°F–72°F	54°F–68°F	50°F–63°F	45°F–55°F
Weather	☀	🌧	🌧	☀	☀	☀

WHAT TO DO/SEE IN FALL

Tokyo Game Show (four days starting on the third Thursday of September)
A huge video game event that takes place in Chiba.

Halloween (October 31)
This familiar holiday takes on new proportions in Tokyo, particularly in Shiba, where enormous crowds gather to celebrate all night long.

Kōyō [koh-oh-yoh-oh] (October and November)
The Japanese love changing autumn leaves as much as they love cherry blossoms in the spring. Maple and ginkgo trees in the parks turn a brilliant red and yellow, offering an ephemeral but striking display.

Tori no ichi* [toh-lee no ee-chee] (November)
This Festival of the Rooster is held two or three times during the month, an opportunity for Japanese people to buy a new kumade [koo-mah-day]—a decorative bamboo rake that brings luck—from Ōtori-jinja shrine in the Asakusa district for the New Year.

Credit: Yoshikazu TAKADA

Christmas lights (starting in late November)

Credit: Tokyo convention and visitor bureau

DRESSING FOR THE WEATHER

September 16–October 15

Typhoon season, the rainy season at summer's end. Winter coats and raincoats are a must, though you'll get the occasional sunny day. Wear long pants and skirts and long-sleeved shirts.

October 16–November 15

Temperatures drop rapidly during this period, but the weather remains mild. Bring cardigans, sweaters, jeans, and light tights.

November 16–30

See next page.

⚠ ***NOTE!**
This event is based on the Chinese calendar. The date varies from year to year. Check the exact date ahead of time while planning your trip.

TOKYO IN **WINTER**

	Dec. 1–15	Dec. 16–31	Jan. 1–15	Jan. 16–31	Feb. 1–15	Feb. 16–28
Average temperature	41°F–55°F	37°F–50°F	36°F–50°F	36°F–50°F	37°F–52°F	39°F–55°F
Weather	☀	☀	❄	❄	❄	☀

DRESSING FOR THE WEATHER

Tokyo winters are relatively mild. Temperatures rarely drop below 32°F and the climate is relatively dry, making snow a rarity. Bring scarves, hats, coats, sweaters, long pants, and thick tights.

Credit: ranpie

Credit: lasta29

TIP!

Major clothing stores carry warm clothing lines (for example, Heat Tech by Uniqlo), but you can also buy handwarmers at konbini or pharmacies. They're called kairo カイロ [ky-roh].

NOTE!

Cold, dry weather can cause dry skin and chapped lips. Bring lip balm and moisturizer.

WHAT TO DO/SEE IN WINTER

Christmas lights (until December 25)

New Year

Temples literally ring in the New Year by ringing the bell 108 times. The Japanese kick off the celebration by visiting a temple at midnight.

Firefighter Parade (January 6)

Firefighters display their equipment and put on a show.

Seijin no Hi (second Monday in January)

A national holiday honoring those who have turned 20, the age of adulthood. Women wear a special kimono for the occasion and men wear suits. At nightfall, they celebrate adulthood by partying in bars, where they are now allowed to drink.

Setsubun (February 3)

A customary celebration where demons are driven out of homes by throwing dried soybeans.

St. Valentine's Day (February 14)

Women traditionally give chocolate to the men in their lives, from significant others to coworkers. In the two or three weeks leading up to the holiday, stores begin selling every kind of chocolatey treat imaginable.

Credit: Korona Lacasse

FOR **FAMILIES**

Like New York City, Tokyo never sleeps. As a result, it can be overstimulating for little ones, especially if they're already jet-lagged. Here are some tips to make life a little easier.

Vary your activities throughout the day. For instance, if you visit a temple in the morning, do something physically active in the afternoon.

> **⚠ NOTE!**
> Avoid the subway during rush hours (8 a.m.–9 a.m. and 5 p.m.–6 p.m.).

Credit: Olivier Bruchez

TAKE **BREAKS**

Pack comfortable shoes for the kids. You'll be walking a lot and waiting in lines, sometimes for hours at a time. Take breaks to let kids run around (at a park or playground), play (batting cages), or explore an arcade.

> **👍 TIP!**
> Pack Velcro shoes for little kids. They'll make your life easier at establishments where you're expected to remove your shoes.

UNIQUE ACTIVITIES

Find a hands-on activity your kids can enjoy. Here is just a sampling of things to do in Tokyo:

- Sculpt candy into animals
- Learn to play the traditional taiko drums
- Learn how to make the realistic plastic food displayed at restaurants
- Drive a subway simulator
- Tale an origami class

OPPORTUNITIES FOR **GROWTH**

Tokyo is an extremely safe city, where children as young as seven walk to school alone and take public transit. You can spot them by their yellow hats. This might be a good opportunity for growth for your kids. Encourage young ones to take initiative, teach preteens to budget spending in a city full of tempting purchases, and introduce kids of all ages to new and exciting flavors.

> **⚠ NOTE!**
> If your kids are responsible and independent, you can split up for a few hours. Just make sure:
> - To agree on a time and place to regroup. If you choose a train station, specify the entrance.
> - Each group has a phone and pocket Wi-Fi device so you can contact each other. A charged power bank is also a good idea.

> **👍 TIP!**
> Tokyo is full of fun interactive museums perfect for kids, including the Toy Museum, Trick Art Museum, and Unko Museum of poop! Children's tickets are discounted or even free.

> **⚠ NOTE!**
> Ghibli Museum tickets cannot be purchased at the door. If you didn't buy tickets ahead of time, don't even bother going. You won't be able to get in.

MEALS

Family restaurants (Jonathan's, Royal Host, Gusto) have their perks:

- Tables that accommodate large groups
- A variety of Western dishes for picky eaters
- Soda fountains
- A good selection of desserts
- Relatively inexpensive

Famiresu: Short for

Family restaurant

ファミレス

famiresu
[fah-mee-lay-soo]

Credit: Marko Kudjerski

Credit: Wing1990hk

> **TIP!**
>
> If you're traveling with babies or toddlers, check out Baby King Kitchen. It's part restaurant, part daycare center.

THEME PARKS

It's a good idea to set aside some time during the trip specifically to do something the kids want to do. It can be a surprise or a deliberate family decision made with their input. Theme parks offer a half or full day of fun for all ages and provide conveniences for little ones. The most popular are:

Tokyo DisneySea
Considered by many to be the best theme park in the world.

Sanrio Puroland
A Hello Kitty–themed park.

Tokyo Dome City
Features a roller coaster that passes through a hole in a building.

Hayanashiki
The city's oldest theme park.

> **TIP!**
>
> Many parks have two pricing systems. Sometimes you can combine them to save money.
>
> The package rate gives you full access to all attractions. Alternatively, you can buy tickets separately for each attraction.
>
> A discounted afternoon or evening price is offered three or four hours before the park closes.

> **NOTE!**
>
> If your kids meet the description below, they might attract attention from locals, especially women, who may ask to take a picture with them:
>
> - Age 12 or under
> - Blond or light brown hair, especially if curly
> - Blue or green eyes
>
> If you don't want the pictures to be posted on social media, just say:
>
> ## NO SNS
> ## をください
>
> No SNS o kudasai
> [no S-N-S oh koo-dah-sy]

Credit: Aimaimyi

FOR **ADULTS ONLY**

Like any major city, Tokyo offers plenty of adult entertainment. But some require you to remain alert.

NOTE!

You must be 20 to buy or consume alcohol or cigarettes, even if you're a tourist.

LOVE **HOTEL**

Japan's tiny apartments and thin walls make intimacy awkward for young lovers and even parents. Love hotels are common in Japan for those private moments.

There are two pricing options:

- Rest: Generally lasting two hours, with an option to purchase extra time in half-hour increments.
- Stay: Staying for the night.

Photos of the rooms are displayed at the entrance. Choose one.

Anonymity is guaranteed. You pay at a machine or at a desk with an opaque window where you only ever see the cashier's hands.

Once in the room, various services are available for free or at an additional cost.

Credit: Karl Baron

PACHINKO

Pachinko machines are a cross between a slot machine and a vertical pinball machine. Thousands of people play them every day for fun. Upon entering a pachinko parlor, you'll be struck by the noise and cigarette smoke. These are an unavoidable part of the experience.

- Each machine is labeled with its win/loss ratio. Choose a winning machine or whichever one appeals to you. The house always wins anyway.
- Insert coins or a bill. A ¥1,000 bill should get you at least ten minutes of play time.
- Retrieve the metal balls and pour them into the designated holder.
- Shoot the balls at the speed and in the direction desired. The goal is to hit specific targets to unlock bonus games to earn more balls.
- When you're out of balls, the game is over.
- If you're lucky or talented enough to accumulate lots of balls, quit while you're ahead. Empty the balls into a container and bring them to the desk to trade them in for a small prize.

TIP!

The Maruhan Shinjuku Toho Building caters to tourists. It's one of the few pachinko parlors with a nonsmoking room.

www.maruhan.co.jp/english/pachinko/

Credit: Tischbeinal

HOSTS AND **HOSTESSES**

In some of the seedier neighborhoods, such as Kabukichō and Roppongi, hawkers on the street try to lure young men into their bars with promises of women known as hostesses. DO NOT GO IN! These bars are owned by the local Mafia and charge outrageous prices for drinks.

Although men have traditionally been the target, single women are now also being offered a fun night with handsome men known as hosts.

TIP!

To spread the net as wide as possible, the Mafia sometimes uses French-speaking hawkers from Africa. If you're addressed in French on the street in Kabukichō, be suspicious.

GAMBLE RESPONSIBLY.

NIGHTCLUBS

NOTE!

Sex work is illegal in Japan, but you might still encounter sex workers scouting for customers at clubs, especially in Roppongi. You might think you impressed that woman on the dance floor, only for her to announce her price later on.

NOTE!

Bring your own condoms from home and make sure they protect against STIs. Some condoms in Japan are only for fun or contraception.

SEX SHOPS

You'll run into more sex shops than you might think. Every Don Quijote store has a restricted adults-only section. Even if it's not your area of interest, it's worth a look around just to check out the innovation and technology.

Credit: Paper ENdipity

LGBTQIA+

Shinjuku-ni-chōme, a few hundred yards east of Kabukichō, is Tokyo's gay district, where queer folk can be out and proud and frequent bars, clubs, and love hotels without judgment. Out of the three hundred or so gay bars, around ten are lesbian bars.

Japan lags far behind the West when it comes to acceptance of LGBTQIA+ people. Although Tokyo is more cosmopolitan and progressive than the rest of Japan (and most Asian capitals), it's still relatively conservative. Some love hotels even refuse to serve same-sex couples, even though such discrimination is illegal. And you'll almost never see same-sex couples holding hands or kissing in public. Public affection by heterosexual couples is considered more acceptable, but avoid excessive PDA (for example, French kissing) nevertheless, as the Japanese are more prudish about such matters.

Subways:

• Shinjuku Sanchōme

• M09 / F13 / S02

• Shinjuku Gyoenmae M10

NOTE!

Some establishments only serve customers who are Japanese or who speak Japanese fluently. Utopia Asia (www.utopia-asia.com/japntoky.htm), an English website, lists tourist-friendly businesses in Tokyo.

Credit: 表示-継承 4.0

TIP!

Visit Tokyo in June if you want to attend Tokyo Pride!
https://pride.tokyo/en/

KEY WORDS AND PHRASES

ARCADES

Menu
メニュー
menyū
[may-nee-oo]

File
ファイル
fairu
[fy-roo]

Mode
モード
mōdo
[moh-oh-doh]

Settings
設定
せってい
settei
[set-tay]

Option
オプション
opushon
[oh-poo-shon]

Select
選択
せんたく
sentaku
[sen-tah-koo]

Level
レーベル
rēberu
[lay-ay-bay-loo]

Easy
簡単
かんたん
kantan
[kahn-tahn]

Hard
難しい
むずかしい
muzukashī
[moo-zoo-kah-shee-ee]

Start
スタート
sutāto
[soo-tah-toh]

Continue
続き
つづき
tsudzuki
[tsoo-dzoo-kee]

Try again
リトライ
ritorai
[lee-toh-ry]

Can you put it back where it was?
元の位置に戻してください
Moto no ichi ni modoshite kudasai
[mo-toh no ee-chee mo-doh-shee-tay koo-dah-sy]

Where should I aim?
どこを狙えばいいですか?
Doko o neraeba ii desuka ?
[doh-koh oh nay-lah-ay-bah ee-ee day-soo-kah]

The button doesn't work
ボタンが効かないです
Botan ga kikanai desu
[bo-tahn gah kee-kahn-ay day-soo]

The coin is stuck
コインが詰まりました
Koin ga tsumarimashita
[koh-een gah tsoo-mah-ree-mah-shee-tah]

KARAOKE

Scheduled time slot	30 minutes	1 hour	2 hours	Free time
プラン	30分	1時間	2時間	フリータイム
puran	sanjubu	ichi jikan	ni jikan	furii taimu
[poo-lahn]	[sahn-joo-boo]	[ee-chee jee-kahn]	[nee jee-kahn]	[foo-lee-ee ty-moo]

All you can drink

飲み放題

nomihōdai
[no-mee-ho-dye]

Can I have another 30 minutes?

30分追加延長できますか。

Sanju bu enchou dekimasu ka?
[sahn-joo boo en-cho-oh day-kee-mahss kah]

Credit: uka0310

Credit: Craig Anderson

PET CAFÉS

Cat	Dog	Rabbit	Parakeet	Ferret
猫	犬	兎	鸚哥	フェレット
neko	inu	usagi	inko	feretto
[nay-koh]	[ee-noo]	[oo-sah-ghee]	[een-koh]	[feh-let-toh]

Hedgehog	Owl	Reptile	Miniature pig	Otter
ヘッジホッグ	梟	爬虫	マイクロブタ	獺
hejihoggu	fukurō	hachū	micro buta	kawauso
[hay-jee-hog-goo]	[foo-koo-ro-oh]	[hah-choo-oo]	[my-koo-lo boo-tah]	[kah-wah-oo-soh]

Family
家族
kazoku
[kah-zoh-koo]

Parents
両親
ryōshin
[ree-oh-oh-sheen]

Children
子供
kodomo
[ko-doh-mo]

Your mother
母
haha
[ha-ha]

Your father
父
chichi
[chee-chee]

Your wife
妻
tsuma
[tsoo-mah]

Your husband
夫
otto
[oht-toh]

Your daughter
娘
musume
[moo-soo-may]

Your son
息子
musuko
[moo-soo-koh]

Your older sister
姉
ane
[ah-nay]

Your younger sister
妹
imouto
[ee-moh-oh-toh]

Your older brother
兄
ani
[ah-nee]

Your younger brother
弟
otouto
[oh-toh-oh-toh]

Baby
赤ちゃん
aka-chan
[ah-kah-chahn]

Stroller
ベビーカー
baby-car
[bay-bee-car]

Diaper
おむつ
omutsu
[oh-moo-tsoo]

Are you free tonight?
今夜暇ですか？
Konya hima desuka ?
[koh-nee-ah hee-mah day-soo-kah]

What time should we meet?
何時に会いますか？
Nanji ni aimasu ka ?
[nahn-jee nee ay-mah-soo kah]

Where should we meet?
何処で会いますか？
Doko de aimasu ka ?
[doh-koh day ay-mah-soo kah]

Shall we go to___?
…に行きますか？
... ni ikimasu ka ?
[___ nee ee-kee-mah-soo kah]

Movie theater
映画館
eigakan
[ay-gah-kahn]

Nightclub
クラブ
kurabu
[koo-lah-boo]

ENTERTAINMENT

BATTING CAGES

Baseball is nearly as popular in Japan as it is in America, and batting cages are everywhere. Some operate slightly differently from others, depending on their location, size, and brand.

PAY

Pay for a round (or three or seven) at the machine. The cost starts at around ¥300 or ¥400 per round, with discounts the more rounds you buy. One round gets you 20–30 balls. You'll be given a card, tickets, or tokens

SUIT UP

Change into a pair of the shoes provided. Put a glove on your dominant hand, grab a helmet and bat, and head for the cages.

CHOOSE A CAGE

Choose a cage based on whether you're right- or left-handed.

Left	Right
左	右
hidari	migi
[hee-dah-lee]	[mee-ghee]

Credit: 江戸村のとくぞう

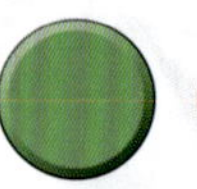 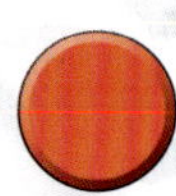

TIP!

All batting cages use the same color code for their buttons:

Green for slow pitches  Red for fast pitches

TIP!

Take a moment to observe the other batters before heading into your cage.

Some places offer cages with predetermined speed and pitch settings to help you train to hit specific pitches.

In any case, most cages let you adjust the pitch speed. Start with the slowest setting (50–55 mph), which is already pretty challenging for amateurs!

Photo TAKA@P.P.R.S

BATTER UP

Insert your card (or ticket or token) into the slot and position yourself in the rectangle on the ground.

A video of a pitcher will play across from you to indicate when the ball is being pitched. At lower-tech centers, a light will come on to tell you that the pitch is coming.

Hit as many balls as you can.

NOTE!

If you want to switch between other members of your party, do so between rounds, and never in the middle of a set. Otherwise, you might get beaned by a ball!

TIP!

Take time to warm up, especially if you've been toting around a heavy backpack all day.

Credit: t.ohashi

TIP!

Tokyo is also home to numerous golf driving ranges, where you can practice your swing. They're usually a little more expensive: an entrance fee of ¥400 to ¥500, plus ¥10 to ¥15 per ball.

Golf practice

練習場

renshuujou
[len-shoo-oo-jo-oh]

BASEBALL GAMES

Japanese people are normally reserved, but they let loose at baseball games! It's an opportunity to see another side of them.

Baseball

野球

yakyū
[yah-kee-yoo-oo]

RULES OF THE GAME

- Baseball is played between two teams of nine players each.

- A game is composed of nine innings. Each inning is divided into two halves, with the teams taking turns batting and fielding.

- As part of the fielding team, the pitcher tries to prevent the batter from hitting the ball. The pitcher must throw the ball into the strike zone, an imaginary rectangle between the batter's shoulders and knees.

- Batters attempt to hit the ball as far as they can to give them time to run around the bases and back to home plate to score a run.

- The fielding team attempts to tag the batter by touching him with the ball or throwing the ball to a teammate on base before the batter can get there.

- If a batter hits the ball out of the field, he has scored a home run. All base runners run around the bases back to home plate.

- If a member of the fielding team catches the ball before it hits the ground, the batter is out.

TEAMS AND SEASONS

Tokyo has two professional baseball teams:

- The Yomiuri Giants, who play at Tokyo Dome (55,000 seats).

- Yakult Swallows, who play at Meiji Jingu Stadium (38,000 seats).

- The season kicks off in late March and ends with playoffs in late October. During the season, there are multiple games every week. Check the calendar on the team or stadium's website.

NOTE!

Some games sell out quickly, such as the one between traditional rivals the Yomiuri Giants and Osaka's Hanshin Tigers.

WHERE TO BUY TICKETS

There are several options:

- Online: On the team or stadium website, which is always available in English. You can pick up your tickets at machines near the box office.

- At the door: Helpful if you want to be able to ask questions.

- Yomiuri Giants box office: Near gate 22 at Tokyo Dome.

- Yakult Swallows box office: Near gate 9 at Meiji Jingu Stadium.

TIP!

If you're ever on the outskirts of Tokyo, there are three other teams whose games you can attend. But be aware: Their websites are only available in Japanese.

Saitama Seibu Lions

Chiba Lotte Marines

Yokohama DeNA BayStars

IN THE STANDS

NOTE!

Baseball games last three or four hours. Despite frequent breaks in action, expect long lines to buy food and drinks.

If you see excitement in the crowd followed by enthusiastic whistling, the ball has landed in the stands. If it's within reach of you, grab it and take a selfie. Then pass the ball to neighboring fans to do the same. An employee will come by soon after to retrieve the ball to avoid fights over it.

You can also take a photo posing with uriko [oo-lee-koh], young women selling beer from mini kegs on their backs during the game.

TIP!

You're allowed to bring in your own drink, but you'll be asked to pour it into a paper cup before entering.

INDOOR SPORTS

Whether you're looking to stay in shape, blow off steam, or simply make use of the facilities available, Tokyo has plenty of opportunities for indoor sports.

PUBLIC GYMS: RECREATION CENTERS

Most city recreation centers offer at least the following:

- A gym (rowing machines, treadmills, weights)
- A dance room (Zumba, Pilates, yoga)
- A martial arts room
- A pool

The great part is that they're quite affordable. Admission for adults costs around ¥400 to ¥600 for access to one or more rooms for three hours. Children are half price, and admission is free for senior citizens and people with disabilities.

TIP!

People in wheelchairs may want to check out the swimming pools, which are equipped with water therapy equipment. Depending on the center, the equipment may be free or cost ¥100.

NOTE!

Bring indoor shoes if you wish to use the gym or dance rooms.

NOTE!

If you have tattoos, you may be offered a wet suit so as not to offend the traditionalists. You're not required to wear them, but doing so will prevent stares.

NOTE!

Some recreation centers are only for neighborhood residents, but the major ones (Shibuya, Shinjuku, Ikebukuro) are open to the public.

GYMS

There are several gym chains in Tokyo, the most popular being Gold's Gym, Anytime Fitness, and Club 360. The first visit is free (any time at Gold's Gym, by appointment at Anytime Fitness), allowing you to try out the machines. Membership costs anywhere between ¥5,000 and ¥6,000.

NOTE!

If you have tattoos, wear long sleeves or pants.

SPORTS CENTERS

It's nearly impossible to list all the kinds of sports centers in Tokyo: Ping-Pong, squash, speed skating, ice-skating, dance. But Tokyo is best known for the number and quality of its rock-climbing centers. It's no surprise that the sport debuted at the 2020 Olympics in Tokyo.

TIP!

The website www.sportsjourney.jp lists the many sports-related opportunities and events available.

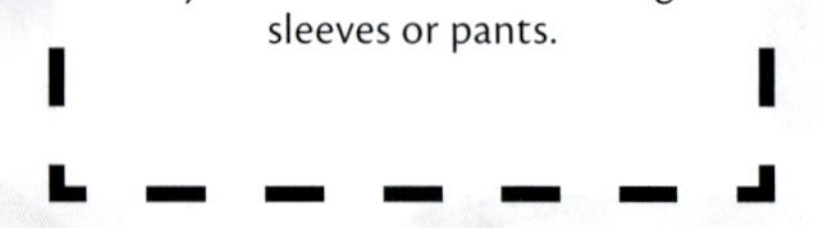

MARTIAL ARTS

Many dojos allow tourists to attend introductory classes. Take the opportunity to check out Japanese martial arts styles that may not be as well-known in the USA as judo or karate.

Aikido

In aikido, the goal is to resolve conflicts peacefully, without attacking, only by turning the attacker's force against him.

Kendo

Kendo is similar to fencing, complete with face mask, but uses a bamboo sword.

Iaido

A Japanese sword art that emphasizes quick reaction times and control in the face of danger.

OUTDOOR SPORTS

In Tokyo, you can play sports, explore, and meet locals all at the same time!

RUNNING

Running is by far the simplest sport to undertake in Tokyo.

Unsurprisingly, city parks (see p. 134) are the best places for a run. Maps are posted at entrances to help you plan your distance and route.

TIP!
Avoid Shinjuku Park, which has an entrance fee. A better bet is Yoyogi Park near Shibuya, where you'll see many Tokyoites also out for a run

TIP!
The path around the Imperial Palace is a popular running route. From dawn to dusk, you'll find Tokyoites happily running alongside tourists.

CYCLING

You can rent electric bikes to get around (see p. 36), but they're also great for jaunts around the city. Various organizations offer half-day or full-day excursions and even provide the bike, safety gear, and English-speaking guide.

Choose from a variety of excursions and price ranges (websites available in English):

Dig Tokyo Tours:
www.digtokyo
tours.com

Y&Y Cycling Tours:
https://cyclingtours
tokyo.com

Soshi's Tokyo Bike Tour:
www.tokyobike
trip.com

Tokyo Great Cycling Tour:
www.tokyocycling.jp

Credit: Toshihiro Gamo

TEAM SPORTS

Many sports clubs allow tourists to jump into a training session or friendly match. You'll typically need to register online in advance.

Search for your favorite sport at www.meetup.com and choose Tokyo as your location.

Once in Tokyo, ask around at tourism offices, the front desk at your hotel, or even neighborhood police stations (kōban) for tips on nearby opportunities.

SUMO WRESTLING

Sumo wrestling is more than just a sport. It's the most notable embodiment of traditional Japanese culture around the world. Here are some tips for exploring this fascinating pastime.

NOTE!

Contrary to what you may have heard, the Japanese don't use the term sumotori for sumo wrestlers. Instead, they're called rikishi [ree-kee-shee].

WHERE TO BUY TICKETS

General admission tickets are available daily at the Ryōgoku Kokugikan arena box office. They're inexpensive (around ¥2,000), but the seats aren't very good.

You can buy reserved seats at any konbini for ¥3,000 to ¥9,000, plus a ¥1,000 reservation fee.

TIP!

You can purchase reserved seats before arriving in Japan at the official Ticket Oosumo website at http://sumo.pia.jp/en (available in English).

NOTE!

If you wish to stay the whole day, spring for the more expensive seats (¥7,000 to ¥8,000) for additional leg room.

NOTE!

If you want to catch the training sessions, you'll have to get up early. They typically take place from 8 a.m. to 12 p.m., and it's best to arrive an hour early.

NOTE!

Heya (sumo stables) are closed to the public during tournaments.

WRESTLING MATCH DATES

If live sumo wrestling is a bucket-list item for you, you have only a narrow range of dates for travel.

Playoffs consist of six tournaments called honbasho that always take place in the second half of odd-numbered months.

Half of the tournaments are held in Tokyo (in January, May, and September), and the other three are held in three different cities around Japan (Osaka in March, Nagoya in July, and Fukuoka in November).

Wrestlers face off in a series of matches from 8 a.m. to 6 p.m. Low-ranked wrestlers compete in the morning. Matches with high-ranked athletes, or yokozuna, begin around three or four o'clock.

TIP!

There aren't many spectators in the morning, making it easy to get closer to the sumo ring (dohyō) to take photos and selfies.

NOTE!

The first and last day of a honbasho are the most popular. Seats sell out in no time.

WHERE TO SEE A MATCH

All Tokyo tournaments are held at Ryōgoku Kokugikan arena (Ryōgoku station, JB21/E12).

WATCHING SUMO TRAINING

If your trip to Japan takes place outside of a tournament period, your only option for a glimpse of the sumo action is to observe a training session. Some heya (sumo stables) allow visitors, but there are strict rules (no talking, no photos, no food or drinks) to prevent spectators from disturbing the athletes.

You must make reservations at least 24 hours in advance, usually by phone. Ask someone at your hotel or at a tourism office to help you.

WELL-KNOWN **STADIUMS**

Tokyo played host to both the 1964 and 2020 Olympics, leaving the city with several stadiums of interest to both sports fans and architecture enthusiasts.

NIPPON BUDOKAN (日本武道館)

Located near the Imperial Palace, the octagonal Nippon Budokan was built for the 1964 Olympics. It is an enormous budokan [boo-doh-kahn], or martial arts arena. But since then, the building has become a premier concert venue, hosting legends from The Beatles in 1966 to Bob Dylan, ABBA, Queen, Prince, Avril Lavigne, and Mariah Carey.

Metro: Kudanshita Station (S 05/Z 06/T 07)

NOTE!
The Budokan is only open to visitors on weekends. Check out the calendar on the arena's website (available in English).

www.nipponbudokan.or.jp/english

RYŌGOKU KOKUGIKAN (両国国技館)

Sumo wrestling tournaments have been held at Tokyo's Ryōgoku Kokugikan arena for decades. Outside of championship periods (see opposite), you can visit the arena at no cost and tour a small museum dedicated to sumo wrestling.

NOTE!
There is very little information in English available at the arena.
Metro: Ryōgoku Station (JB 21/E 12)

www.sumo.or.jp/En

YOYOGI NATIONAL GYMNASIUM (国立代々木競技場)

Designed by architect Kenzō Tange, Yoyogi National Gymnasium in north Shibuya is actually made up of two seashell-shaped buildings that seat 9,000 and 3,000, respectively. Their suspension roofs are supported entirely from the outside so that there are no pillars to block spectators' views indoors. If you aren't able to go inside, you can still appreciate the architecture from a promenade.

Metro: Meiji-jingumae Station (C 03/F 15), Harajuku (JY 19)

www.jpnsport.go.jp
(click English, then Sport Facility)

TOKYO DOME (東京ドーム)

Affectionately nicknamed the Big Egg by Tokyoites, Tokyo Dome is home to the local baseball team the Tokyo Giants. It features an air-supported membrane roof and also serves as a concert venue for some of the biggest names in the business. The 55,000-seat stadium is closed to visitors outside of games and concerts, but a baseball museum details the evolution of the sport in Japan, and there are a number of fun activities available in Tokyo Dome City, the neighborhood surrounding the stadium.

Metro:

Suidōbashi Station (JB 17/I 11),
Kōrakuen Station (M 22/N 11),
Kasuga Station (E 07/I 12)

www.tokyo-dome.co.jp/en/tourists

Credit: 江戸村のとくぞう

TOKYO AQUATICS CENTRE

Built for the 2020 Olympics, this gigantic aquatic complex seats 15,000 and features a modular 50-meter pool that can be converted into two 25-meter pools.

Metro: Tatsumi Station (Y 23), Shiomi Station (JE 04)

MUSIC: **CONCERTS**

With a little effort and exploration, Tokyo can be a dream city for music lovers.

LIVE HOUSES

These small music venues come in all sizes—from the well-known Liquidroom, Unit, and Zepp to hole-in-the-wall joints—and offer music for every taste (rock, jazz, electro, pop). Tokyo Gig Guide is an English website that lists upcoming shows and concerts.

www.tokyogigguide.com/en

Some neighborhoods are known for particular music genres. Find an area with your favorite music.

GENRE	NEIGHBORHOOD
Traditional Japanese music	Asakusa
House/Techno	Shibuya
EDM	Roppongi
J-Pop/Idols	Akihabara
K-Pop	Shin-Ōkubo
Punk	Koenji
Rock	Shimokitazawa
Hip-hop	Harajuku

CONCERT CAFÉS

There are too many concert cafés in Tokyo to list them all. Most are dedicated to jazz. Do some research ahead of time or ask at a tourism office for the best venues.

NOTE!

Most establishments have limited capacity, so try to get there early, especially if the performers are popular.

NOTE!

Most establishments charge an admission fee.

STREET CONCERTS

In Tokyo, street concerts start at the crack of dawn. But unlike in the States, musicians aren't playing for money. Instead, most are hoping to make a name for themselves by selling self-produced CDs or to be discovered by music producers. If you're lucky, you might even stumble across a well-known artist spending an evening going back to their roots and communing with audiences.

The neighborhoods with the most street concerts are:

Shinjuku

South exit	East exit, across from Studio Alta	Southeast exit, at the plaza across from the Gap store

Harajuku	**Ikebukuro**	**Akihabara**	**Ueno**
Street 413, which cuts across Yoyogi Park	East exit of the station	Bus station	Park paths

Shimokitazawa	**Takadanobaba**	**Shibuya**
South exit of the station, under the elevated railway bridge	Around the station, particularly near the mural of Osamu Tezuka's mangas	Plaza in front of the Tokyo College of Music Passage between the Hachikō statue and the Shibuya Mark City Mall

NOTE!

If you're a musician yourself and want to put on your own street concert, check out Guitar Street, which is lined with music stores where you can buy or even rent a guitar to play in the street.

To get there, take the Ochanomizubashi exit at Ochanomizu station and head for Meidaidōri [my-ee-dye-doh-ree], or Meidai Street.

FESTIVALS

If you're traveling in the summer, check out the many music festivals on offer. The two most popular are:

Fuji Rock

Takes place in late July at the foot of Mount Fuji (90 minutes from Tokyo). Attended by 100,000 to 150,000 festivalgoers each year.

Summer Sonic

Held in mid-August, it has grown so large that it now takes place simultaneously in Tokyo and Osaka.

MUSIC: **RECORD STORES**

Tokyo is a gold mine for music lovers seeking to add to their vinyl collection.

Japanese records are famous the world over. The releases tend to be issued in smaller runs than in the USA, the music isn't remastered or remixed so it's closer to the original recording, and the pressing is better quality. Your trip to Tokyo is the perfect opportunity to round out your collection or unearth a hidden gem.

Credit: chinnian

BEST **NEIGHBORHOODS**

Tokyo is littered with record stores. If you look hard enough, you'll almost always find one near a major subway station (particularly Yamanote).

But the two neighborhoods with the most record stores are:

Shibuya

The majority of shops carry mainstream music, from 1970s classics to present-day hits, at a wide range of prices (extremely rare editions go for eye-watering sums).

Shimokitazawa

You'll mostly find indie and experimental albums for discerning hipsters in a narrower price range.

CHAIN **STORES**

You'll almost certainly come across at least one of the numerous indie record shops in Tokyo during your trip, but if you don't want to leave things to chance, try one of the three major chains.

Disk Union

Disk Union has many locations across Tokyo selling a variety of used albums. Each store features a general selection, as well as specialty sections that vary by neighborhood (rock in Shinjuku, house in Shimokitazawa, jazz in Kochijōji).

The best-known Disk Union location in Tokyo is without a doubt the one in Shibuya, where you could spend a whole day digging through bins.

Click the Google Translate tab on the website for an AI-generated English version and to find the company's main locations.

https://diskunion.net/st/shop/

HMV

HMV dominated the market prior to the turn of the century, but its empire has since collapsed, leaving only three surviving stores in Tokyo—in Shibuya, Shinjuku, and Kichijōji—which share an enormous inventory. Head here for original soundtracks for movies and animations (including Ghibli).

www.hmv.co.jp/recordshop/news/

Tower Records

Founded in Sacramento, Tower Records stores can now be found throughout Japan. The eleventh floor of the flagship Shinjuku store is dedicated entirely to records under the Tower Vinyl label. Tablets are provided for quick searches among the 70,000 titles in stock (40,000 used). Ask employees for help in-store and/or for recommendations for other shops in the city.

Japanese only.

https://tower.jp/site/vinyl

NOTE!

Some stores alphabetize records by the Roman alphabet and others by the Japanese alphabet.

Credit: Corpse Reviver

BOOKSTORES

The Japanese have had a love affair with literature for centuries. Between the city's major bookstore retailers and secondhand bookshops, Tokyo is a bookworm's idea of heaven.

BOOKSTORE CHAINS

Here are just a few of the nationwide bookstore chains with multiple locations in Tokyo.

Kinokuniya

The main location has a vast selection of foreign language books (including English) on the seventh floor.

www.kinokuniya.co.jp/c/store/Books-Kinokuniya-Tokyo

Metro: Shinjuku (East exit)

Tsutaya

The main location stocks over 60,000 books on art and sells traditional souvenirs, including katanas.

https://store.tsite.jp/ginza/english/

Metro: Ginza

Daikanyama

Daikanyama's store houses a cozy café, a relaxing spot to enjoy a book. The trees surrounding the shop give it the feel of a forest amid the city.

https://store.tsite.jp/daikanyama/english/

Metro: Daikanyama, Nakameguro

Maruzen Marunouchi

Likely the largest bookstore in the city, with over 200,000 items. But manga fans should visit the Nihonbashi location, which specializes in graphic novels.

www.marunouchi.com/tenants/2015

Metro: Tokyo (Marunouchi North exit)

Yaesu Book Center

In addition to its nine stories of books of all kinds, the store keeps bees on the roof of the building, and the café offers a number of honey-flavored treats.

www.yaesu-book.co.jp (in Japanese)

Metro: Tokyo (Yaesu exit), Kyōbashi

TIP!

Because the Japanese are meticulous about handwriting, most bookstores also include a well-stocked stationery section.

SECONDHAND BOOKSTORES

With over 150 secondhand bookshops, the Jimbōchō district is a veritable bonanza for collectors. There's everything from well-worn books at a pittance to limited editions at stupefying prices.

There are too many shops to list, but here are two that are worth checking out:

Ohya Shobo

Carries one of the largest collections of eighteenth- and nineteenth-century prints and illustrated books.

www.ohya-shobo.com/english/

Kitazawa Bookstore

Founded in 1902, Kitazawa Bookstore specializes in academic works and has archives of centuries-old texts, as well as an impressive number of books in English.

www.kitazawa.co.jp/kindex.html

Metro: Jimbōchō

LIBRARIES

Some wards have public libraries. The size of their inventory varies, but in any case, they make a good spot to get out of the rain! Two in particular stand out:

Credit: Wiiii

International Library of Children's Literature

The only library in all of Japan to carry only children's books—over 400,000 of them.

www.kodomo.go.jp/en/

Metro: Uguisudani/Ueno

National Diet Library

Located next to the Diet (Japanese parliament), the library owns an impressive collection of documents (books, maps, laws) related to Japan's history.

www.ndl.go.jp/en

Metro: Nagatachō, Kokkaigijidomae

BOOK OFF

Leading secondhand book retailer Book Off has sixty locations in Tokyo, where you'll find complete manga collections, photobooks of Japanese celebrities, and other art books at affordable prices. The Japanese generally treat their books with care, so even used books are like new.

www.bookoff.co.jp/inbound/index.html#tokyo

Credit: Corpse Reviver

Credit: 運転太郎

TIP!

Books are heavy. Buying too many might cause you to exceed your airline's luggage weight limit for the flight home. The solution? Mail them to yourself! Like the US postal system, the Japanese post office offers a media mail rate for books and magazines.

Media mail rate

印刷物

insatsu butsu
[een-sat-soo boo-tsoo]

- Choose the size of your box (or tube for posters): small, medium, or large.
- The employee will verify that you're only sending books and magazines in your package.
- If your package exceeds the weight limit, you may have to send multiple packages.
- Choose the shipping method. Shipping by boat is cheaper than airmail but almost as fast. Your package should arrive in approximately ten days.

Whatever you pay, you can tell yourself that it would've cost twice that to check an additional bag at the airport!

FASHION

Whatever your style or budget, Tokyo is the fashion capital of Asia and a fashionista's paradise—if you know where to look.

THE **GOLDEN TRIANGLE**

The epicenter of Tokyo fashion is located between Harajuku, Shibuya, and Omotesandō stations. You could easily spend a full day there exploring the seventeen-acre district.

Harajuku

A mecca for all things kawaii [kah-wy-ee], the Japanese word for cute. Mainly frequented by teenage girls.

TIP!
Lovers of vintage styles gather at Yoyogi Park on Sunday mornings to show off their rockabilly and Victorian outfits. Ask for permission before taking photos.

Takeshita Street is a nearby iconic pedestrian street, but only tourists go there nowadays. Many of the shops sell mainly souvenir clothing. Check out the side streets instead, where you'll find more artisan shops.

Credit: IQRemix

The street is easily visible from the subway station, thanks to the entrance arch decorated with a design (which changes every season) made of plastic balloons.

TIP!
If the crowds are making you claustrophobic, take the side street next to the Marion Crêpes stand, continue about ten meters, and take the stairs on your right. They lead to Togo Jinja, a small shrine where you can take a breather.

Omotesandō

Omotesandō Avenue is comparable to Fifth Avenue in New York City. It stretches from Laforet Harajuku for three-quarters of a mile to Omotesandō station. The shops lining the street include both international brands (Balmain, Louis Vuitton, Vivienne Westwood) and Japanese ones (Kenzo, Issey, Miyake) displaying haute couture trends for both men and women.

Credit: K

TIP!
Streets parallel to Omotesandō Avenue are filled with clothing thrift stores and bazaar stalls.

Shibuya

If Harajuku is for girls, Shibuya is for women, the district where fashionable twenty-something Tokyoites shop at the department store called 109 (ichi-maru-kyu) [ee-chee-mah-loo-kee-oo]. Its smaller offshoot, 109 Men, suggests that the district is starting to offer menswear as well.

TIP!
Parco [pah-loo-koh] Mall is especially tourist-friendly.

TIP!
Don't limit yourself to local brands. International brands often sell items exclusively available in Japan that you can't get back home.

Credit: Tokyo convention and visitor bureau

OTHER **OPTIONS**

GINZA

Ginza is the luxury district, located south of Tokyo station. If Omotesandō Avenue is similar to Fifth Avenue, then Ginza is like Los Angeles's Rodeo Drive, with luxury malls full of high-end brands. The architecture alone is worth a look around.

KOENJI

Located west of Shinjuku, Koenji is a boho neighborhood teeming with vintage shops. The countless thrift stores sell clothes in retro styles, particularly from the 1960s and 1970s—although some of the shops have been around since the 1920s!

Credit: nakashi

TIP!
Chuo-dori, Ginza's main artery, is reserved for pedestrians only on weekends and holidays from noon to 5 p.m. (or 6 p.m. from April to September).

SHIMOKITAZAWA

Located a couple miles west of Shibuya, Shimokitazawa is another bohemian district but is noticeably calmer. The side streets are overflowing with boutiques by young artisans, as well as thrift stores of every kind.

UENO

Several stores along Ameya Yokochō specialize in US army surplus goods, which were sold on the black market after World War II. The street is nicknamed Ameyoko and can by spotted by the arch at its entrance bearing its name: アメ横.

Credit: keyaki

TECH

Japan has been known for its cutting-edge technology since the 1970s. Your trip is an opportunity for you to pick up equipment for your hobby (or for work) at low prices.

CHAINS

There are two nationwide chains with tens of store locations in Tokyo: Bic Camera and Yodobashi.

They carry all things electronic and electronics-related for everything from household appliances to computers to phones and cameras.

In the more touristy areas, the multistory buildings employ English-speaking staff to help customers.

Both companies also offer a 10% tax exemption on purchases over ¥5,000 (see p. 47).

TIP!

Within a day or so of arriving, purchase electronics accessories for use during your trip: USB adapters, voltage transformers, power banks, and digital cameras. Take a moment to browse for deals on items to buy at the end of your trip—budget permitting, that is.

Credit: Joakim Jardenberg

NOTE!

Many rebates are given in the form of a store card. Check with an employee before paying.

NOTE!

The Japanese mobile phone market is dominated by Apple, so the majority of accessories are made for iPhones.

AKIHABARA

The electronics district attracts millions of tourists annually. Avoid the stores on the main streets at all costs. By exploring the narrow side streets, you'll find the best deals in three areas:

Data storage

Tiny outlet stores sell flash cards, SD cards, USB drives, and memory sticks.

Hardware

DIY electronics builders will find everything they need, from capacitors to fans to cables.

Photography

In Japan, home of Canon and Nikon, you'll find new and used lenses at prices other countries can only dream of. But take the time to price shop.

TIP!

The staff rarely speak English, so if there's an item in a display case that you want, take a picture of it with your phone and show it to an employee.

TIP!

The farther away from the subway station, the lower the prices.

Metro: Akihabara JY 03 – JB 19 – JK 28 – H 15

Credit: Paul Bou

FOR THE KITCHEN

Tokyo offers quite a few irresistible ingredients and equipment for foodies and serious cooks.

Credit: 運転太郎

CONDIMENTS

There's nothing like local condiments and seasoning to give your cooking that authentic Japanese zing. Plus, they're small and nonperishable, making them easy to stuff in a suitcase. Here are some daily essentials you can find at any mini-mart.

Soy sauce

醤油

shōyu
[sho-oh-yoo]

Seven spice

七味唐辛子

shichimi togarashi
[shit-shi-mi to-gara-shi]

Sichuan pepper

山椒

sanshō
[sahn-sho-oh]

Ponzu sauce

ポン酢

ponzu
[pohn-zoo]

Curry
(sold in cubes to dissolve in hot water)

カレー

kare
[kah-lay-ay]

EQUIPMENT

Kappabashi

Kappabashi Street in the Asakusa district is lined with restaurant supply stores that also sell to tourists. Although it's a good distance from the subway, you can't miss the giant statue of a mustachioed chef outside the south entrance.

Take the time to explore the whole street before making any purchases to make sure you don't miss the specialty shops for things like bakeware, knives, and dishware.

Metro: Tawaramachi G 18

Kappabashi Street

合羽橋通り

kappabashi-dōri
[kahp-pah-bah-shee-doh-oh-lee]

100-yen shops (see pg. 104)

Some 100-yen store chains specialize in kitchen equipment. They're smaller than their generalist counterparts. Two brands stand out:

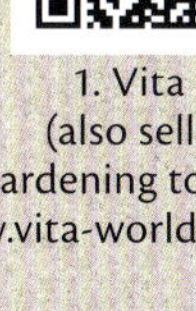

1. Vita
(also sells gardening tools):
www.vita-world.jp/shop

2. Natural Kitchen:
www.natural-kitchen.jp

Credit: City Foodster

PARKS

With all the noise in Tokyo and an urban landscape stretching as far as the eye can see, it's nice to take time to unwind amid nature. You can do so by strolling around one of the splendid city parks.

NOTE!
Parks swarm with locals during cherry blossom season (hanami) from late March to early April. Arrive extra early to avoid long lines.

Credit: Kakidai

YOYOGIKŌEN (代々木公園)

Yoyogi Park sits next to Shibuya and is popular with locals. It offers something for everyone. You can run, play on the grass, do some yoga, rent a bike and enjoy the bike paths, admire the foliage, or grab a drink with friends.

On Sunday mornings, groups put on public performances of their favorite pastimes: martial arts, cosplay, rockabilly music, juggling, and dancing.

Credit: Shinjiro

UENO PARK (上野公園)

The most popular park in Tokyo, with several museums and a zoo that is home to two pandas, the district's pride and joy as well as its mascots.

SHINJUKU GYOEN
NATIONAL GARDEN (新宿御苑)

This emerald of a park is divided into three distinct gardens: a French-style garden with a giant rose garden, an English-style garden with a greenhouse, and a traditional Japanese garden.

Shinjuku Gyoen is the only park in central Tokyo that charges an admission fee (¥500, but free for kids 15 and under).

NOTE!
Try to go in the morning, if possible, as soon as the park opens at 9 a.m. It closes early in winter and late in summer: 4:30 p.m. in fall and winter, 6 p.m. from March to September, and 7 p.m. in July and August.

TIP!
Scan the QR code for a free English audio guide.

www.env.
go.jp/garden/
shinjukugyoen/english

MEIJI JINGŪ (明治神宮)

This Shinto shrine lies north of Yoyogi Park amid a forest of a hundred thousand trees. Walk down a path lined with enormous sake barrels and wine casks to arrive at the shrine's stunning courtyard.

On weekends, you may see couples getting married in the Shinto tradition. You may take photos of the ceremony as long as you respect the lovebirds' special day.

Credit: vr4msbfr

IMPERIAL PALACE GARDENS (皇居東御苑)

Credit: Daria Focht

Only the gardens on the east side of the palace grounds are open to the public. You'll have to go through security.

Exit on the north side through the Kita-hanebashi-mon gate (江戸城 北桔橋門). Past the bridge is Kitanomaru Park (北の丸公園), which offers a more tranquil atmosphere.

KEY WORDS AND **PHRASES**

BATTING CAGES

Batting center
バッティング
センター
battingu centā
[bat-tin-goo sen-tah-ah]

Driving range
練習場
renshuujou
[len-shoo-oo-jo-oh]

Credit: TAKA@P.P.R.S

BASEBALL GAME

Game
試合
shiai
[shee-ay]

Team
チーム
team
[chee-moo]

Player
選手
senshu
[sen-shoo]

Win
勝ち
kachi
[kah-chee]

Loss
負け
make
[mah-kay]

Tie
引き分け
hikiwake
[hee-kee-wah-kay]

INDOOR SPORTS

Gymnastics
体操
taisō
[ty-soh-oh]

Table tennis
卓球
takkyū
[tak-kee-oo-oo]

Swimming
水泳
suiei
[soo-ee-ay]

Ice-skating
アイススケート
aisu sukēto
[ay-soo skay-toh]

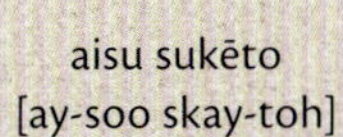

OUTDOOR SPORTS

Sports
スポーツ
supotsu
[soo-poh-tsoo]

Baseball
野球
yakyū
[yah-kee-yoo-oo]

Soccer
サッカー
soccer
[sahk-kah-ah]

Tennis
テニス
tenisu
[tay-nee-soo]

Golf
ゴルフ
gorufu
[go-loo-foo]

Basketball
バスケット
ボール
basuketto boru
[bah-soo-ket-toh
bo-loo]

Volleyball
バレー
ボール
barēbōru
[bah-lay-ay-bo-
oh-loo]

Rugby
ラグビー
ragubī
[rah-goo-bee-ee]

Football
アメフト
amefuto
[ah-may-foo-toh]

MARTIAL ARTS

Kendo
剣道
kendō
[ken-doh-oh]

Judo
柔道
jūdō
[joo-oo-doh-oh]

Karate
空手
karate
[kah-rah-tay]

Aikido
合気道
aikidō
[ay-ee-kee-doh-oh]

Iaido
居合道
iaidō
[ee-ay-ee-doh-oh]

Kyudo
弓道
kyūdō
[kyoo-oo-doh-oh]

Credit: Ignat Gorazd

EXERCISE

Exercise
運動
undou
[oon-doh-oh]

Cycling
サイクリング
saikuringu
[sy-koo-lin-goo]

Running
ランニング
ranningu
[rahn-nin-goo]

Jogging
ジョギング
jogingu
[jo-ging-oo]

I play___
___をします
___o shimasu
[___ oh shee-mahss]

SUMO

Sumo wrestling
相撲
sumō
[soo-moh]

Sumo wrestler
力士
rikishi
[ree-kee-shee]

Main tournament
本場所
honbasho
[hon-bah-sho]

Sumo ring
土俵
dohyo
[doh-hee-yo]

BASEBALL - EQUIPMENT

Helmet
打撃用ヘルメット
dageki-yo herumetto
[dah-gay-kee-yo heh-loo-met-toh]

(Baseball) bat
(野球用)バット
(yakyū-yo) batto
[(yah-kee-yoo-oo) bat-toh]

Ball (for baseball)
(野球)ボール
(yakyū) bōru
[(yah-kee-yoo-oo) bo-oh-loo]

(Baseball) glove
野球グローブ
(yakyū) gurōbu
[(yah-kee-yoo-oo) goo-oh-oh-boo]

Batting glove
バッティンググローブ
battingu gurōbu
[bat-ting-oo goo-loh-oh-boo]

BASEBALL - FIELD

Diamond
ダイヤモンド
daiyamondo
[dy-ah-mon-doh]

Infield
内野
naiya
[nah-ee-yah]

Outfield
外野
gaiya
[gah-ee-yah]

Base
本塁
honrui
[hon-roo-ee]

Home run
本塁
honruida
[hon-roo-ee-dah]

RECORD STORES

CD
シーディー
shīdī
[shee-ee-dee-ee]

Record
ビニール
binīru
[bee-nee-ee-loo]

Album
アルバム
alubamu
[ah-loo-bahm]

Single
シングル
shinguru
[sheen-goo-loo]

Song
歌
uta
[oo-tah]

Title
曲名
kyokumei
[kee-oh-koo-may]

Artist
歌手
kashu
[kah-shoo]

Classical music
クラシック
kurashikku
[koo-lah-sheek-koo]

Rock
ロック
rokku
[lohk-koo]

Pop
ポップ
poppu
[pop-poo]

J-pop
J-Pop
[jay pop-poo]

Hip hop
ヒップホップ
hippu hoppu
[heep-poo hop-poo]

Electronic music
電子音楽
denshi ongaku
[den-shee ohn-gah-koo]

I'm looking for music by ___. Do you have it?
___ のおんがくをさがしているのですが、ありますか？
___ no ongaku o sagashite iru no desu ga, arimasu ka?
[___ no ohn-gah-koo oh sah-gah-shee-tay ee-loo no day-soo gah ah-lee-mahss kah]

BOOKSTORES

Bookstore
書店
shoten
[sho-ten]

OR

Bookstore
本屋
honya
[hon-yah]

Book
本
hon
[hon]

Old book
古本
furuhon
[foo-loo-hon]

Stationery
文房具
bunbōgu
[boon-bo-oh-goo]

Photography
写真
shashin
[sha-sheen]

Poster
ポスター
posutā
[poh-soo-tah-ah]

Drawing
描
ka
[kah]

Magazine
雑誌
zasshi
[zah-Ø-shi]

Print
浮世絵
ukiyo-e
[oo-kee-yo-ay]

Picture book
絵本
ehon
[ay-hon]

Children's book
児童書
jidō-sho
[jee-doh-oh-sho]

Author
著者
chosha
[sho-shah]

TECH

USB drive
USBフラッシュ
ドライブ

USB Flash Drive
[yoo-ess-bee foo-lah-shoo doh-ry-boo]

Memory card
メモリーカード

Memory Card
[may-moh-ree-ee kah-ah-doh]

Power bank
モバイル
バッテリー

Mobile Battery
[moh-by ba-teh-ree-ee]

Digital camera
デジタルカメラ

Digital Camera
[dee-jee-tah-loo kah-may-rah]

Lens
レンズ

lense
[len-zoo]

Flash
ストロボ

strobe
[soo-toh-loo-bo]

Camcorder
ビデオカメラ

Video Camera
[bee-day-oh kah-may-rah]

AC adapter
ACアダプタ

AC Adapter
[ay-see ah-dah-poo-tah]

PARKS AND **NATURE**

Park
公園

kōen
[koh-oh-en]

Tree
木

ki
[kee]

Flower
花

hana
[hah-nah]

Nature
自然

shizen
[shee-zen]

Grass
草

kusa
[koo-sah]

KITCHEN

Kitchen knife
包丁

hōchō
[ho-oh-choh-oh]

Cutting board
まな板

manaita
[mah-nah-ee-tah]

Plate
お皿

osara
[oh-sah-rah]

Chopsticks
お箸

ohashi
[oh-hah-shee]

Long cooking chopsticks
菜箸

saibashi
[sy-bah-shee]

Whisk
泡立て器

awatadeki
[ah-wah-tah-day-kee]

MINOR EMERGENCIES

FIRST **AID**

Minor injuries and illnesses can crop up at any time during your trip.
A pharmacy will have almost everything you need.

NOTE!

If you experience a serious injury or severe symptoms, contact St. Luke's International Hospital immediately. Or go to the emergency room if needed.

9-1 Akashi-cho,
Chuo-ku,
Tokyo 104-8560

Telephone:
03-5550-7166

https://hospital.
luke.ac.jp/eng/for-
patients

Pharmacy

薬局

yakkyoku
[yak-kee-oh-koo]

DESCRIBING YOUR **SYMPTOMS**

I have a fever
熱があります
Netsu ga arimasu
[net-soo gah ah-lee-mahss]

I don't feel well
具合 が 悪い です
Guai ga warui desu
[goo-ay gah wah-roo-ee day-soo]

My ___ hurts
___が 痛い です
___ga itai desu
[___ gah ee-ty day-soo]

Head
頭
atama
[ah-tah-mah]

Teeth
歯
ha
[ha]

Eye
目
me
[may]

Ear
耳
mimi
[mee-mee]

Hand
手
te
[tay]

Wrist
手首
tekubi
[tay-koo-bee]

Elbow
肘
hiji
[hee-jee]

Throat
喉
nodo
[no-doh]

Stomach
お腹
onaka
[oh-nah-kah]

Knee
膝
hiza
[hee-zah]

Ankle
足首
ashikubi
[ah-shee-koo-bee]

Foot/Leg
足
ashi
[ah-shee]

I have diarrhea
下痢があります
Geri ga arimasu
[gay-ree gah ah-lee-mahss]

I'm constipated
便秘です
Benpi desu
[ben-pee day-soo]

I'm bleeding
出血
が あります
Shukketsu ga arimasu
[shoo-Ø-ket-soo gah ah-
lee-mahss]

Injury
きず
kizu
[kee-zoo]

**I'm having an
allergic reaction**
アレルギー
が でました
Arerugi ga demashita
[ah-lay-loo-ghee gah day-
mah-shee-tah]

OVER-THE-COUNTER **DRUGS**

NOTE!
Japanese dosages are sometimes higher than in the United States. Check with the pharmacist.

What is the dosage?
何の用量？
Nani no yōrō?
[nah-nee no yoh-oh-loh-oh]

How often?
どの周波数？
Dono shūhasū?
[doh-noh shoo-oo-ha-shoo-oo]

PAINKILLERS

BUFFERIN バファリン

Comes in four varieties: Bufferin A (classic), Bufferin Premium (severe pain), Bufferin Luna (muscle pain), and Bufferin Kaze Ex (flu-like symptoms).

EVE イブ

Comes in three varieties: EVE A (classic), EVE A EX (severe pain), EVE Quick DX (migraines).

LOXONIN S ロキソニン S

Stronger than the other two brands but can cause upset stomach.

Credit: Yoshi 2012

TIP!
Some painkillers are particularly effective for menstrual cramps. If you find one you like, buy several boxes to take home!

COLD AND FLU

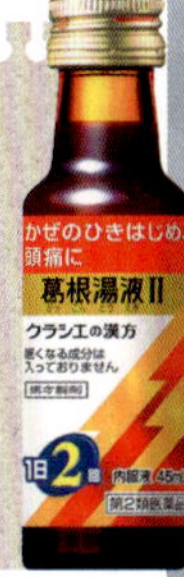

PABULON パブロン
Sore throat, runny nose.

LULU ATTACK EX ルルアタックEX
Fever, achiness, dizziness.

KAKKONTO 葛根湯
A blend of medicinal herbs to soothe all flu-like symptoms.

DIGESTIVE ISSUES

OHTA ISAN 太田胃散
Nausea, vomiting, acid reflux, hangovers. Made with medicinal herbs.

SEIROGAN 正露丸
Diarrhea, loose stools, food poisoning, toothaches.

Credit: Ohta Isan

PERSONAL CARE

Sunburn 日焼け
hiyake
[hee-yah-kay]

Sunscreen 日焼け止め
hiyakedome
[hee-yah-kay-doh-may]

Bandages 絆創膏
bansōkō
[bahn-so-oh-koh-oh]

TIP!
If you have young kids, stock up on cute bandages for ouchies back home.

BUG BITES

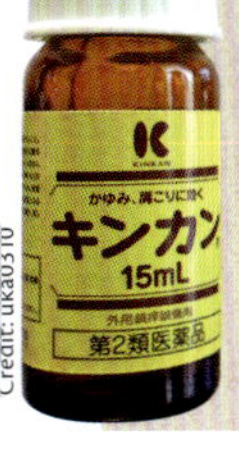

KINKAN キンカン
Sold in liquid form with an eyedropper.

MUHI ムヒ
Sold as cream in a tube.

Credit: DocChewbacca

BROKEN **EYEGLASSES**

If you break your eyeglasses or lose your contact lens case, don't panic! Here's what you can do.

Zoff and Jins are two chain stores that can make new eyeglasses for you in one hour starting at ¥5,000. They even offer tax exemptions.

Zoff

www.zoff.co.jp

Jins

www.jins.com/jp

TIP!
Search for a store located in or near a touristy area to increase your chances of finding an employee who speaks English.

Glasses
メガネ
megane
[may-gah-nay]

Contact lenses
コンタクトレンズ
contact lenses
[kon-tah-koo-too len-zoo]

I broke my glasses
メガネを壊した
megane wo kowashita
[may-gah-nay oh koh-wah-shee-tah]

I lost my glasses
メガネをなくした
megane wo nakushita
[may-gah-nay oh nah-koo-shee-tah]

I'd like to buy some glasses
メガネを買いたい
megane wo kaitai
[may-gah-nay oh ky-ty]

Credit: chinnian

CONTACT **LENSES**

Both Zoff and Jins sell packs of daily contact lenses. If they don't have your prescription in stock, you'll have to come back the next day.

BLUE LIGHT GLASSES

If you have twenty-twenty vision but spend a lot of time working on screens, pick up a pair of blue-light glasses, which filter out blue light. They're widely available, particularly at electronics stores.

AT THE **OPTOMETRIST**

Step 1
Choose a pair of frames. Some stores sell inexpensive (¥3,000) frames that are good enough to get by with.

Step 2
Get your eyes tested. Instead of the usual eye chart with letters, Japan uses circles pointing in different directions. If you can't remember the names of the directions, you can always point with your finger.

Step 3
Choose optional extras for your lenses (extra thin lenses, blue-light filters, progressive lenses). But skip them if you need the glasses right away, as these features can take a few days.

UP
ue
[oo-ay]

LEFT
hidari
[hee-dah-lee]

RIGHT
migi
[mee-ghee]

DOWN
shita
[shee-tah]

Your new glasses will be ready in thirty minutes. Choose from among the free cases and lens wipes and you're on your way!

TIP!
If you want to keep your old frames, the store can measure them and make new lenses to fit.

EARTHQUAKES

While highly unlikely, it's not impossible for a major earthquake to occur during your stay. Here's what you should do.

Japan sits at the intersection of four tectonic plates, resulting in tiny but frequent earthquakes, over a thousand each year. You may experience an earthquake during your trip. The vast majority of the time, they're brief and inconsequential. At most, trains and elevators might automatically pause for a moment.

MAJOR EARTHQUAKES

NOTE!
It's worth repeating: The situation described below is **HIGHLY UNLIKELY**. But if it does occur, whatever you do, don't panic!

AT THE MALL

- Elevators are programmed to stop at the nearest floor at the slightest quake. Get out.
- Walk, don't run.
- Follow staff instructions.
- If necessary, take cover under a table or other heavy furniture.

IN THE STREET

- Cover your head with a purse or rolled-up jacket for protection.
- Get away from buildings. The greatest danger is falling glass. Stay away from utility poles, too.
- Follow the crowd but don't run. Locals know the safest places to wait it out—usually newer buildings.

IN A CAR

- Pull over to the left side of the road and turn off the car.
- Stay in your vehicle. If you must get out, leave the door open and the keys in the ignition.

NOTE!
The Bōsaikan risk prevention center near the Ikebukuro fire station offers free simulations of smoke-filled hallways, fires, and earthquakes. You can even experience a simulation of the March 2011 earthquake.

INDOORS

- Grab a cushion, pillow, or folded towel and put it over your head for protection.
- Open the doors to prevent being trapped inside.
- Take cover under a table or desk.
- Stay away from windows. Glass is the first thing to break in major earthquakes.

NOTE!
Resist the urge to grab your belongings and make a run for it.

IN THE SUBWAY

- At the slightest quake, the train will stop automatically.
- Hold tight to a handle or pole.
- Follow staff instructions.

AFTERWARD

Call the numbers below if necessary:

110: Police
119: Ambulance

03-3224-5000: US Embassy in Tokyo

Stay hydrated.

Ikebukuro Bōsaikan

池袋防災館

[ee-kay-boo-koo-roh bo-oh-sy-kahn]

https://tokyo-bskan.jp/en/

HELP! I MISSED
THE LAST TRAIN!

You were having too much fun and lost track of time and now you've missed the last train home. Here's what you can do instead.

IF YOUR HOTEL **IS NEARBY**

Walk

The cheapest option and also the slowest. This may or may not be a good option, depending how tired you are and how far you have to go.

Enter the hotel address into Google Maps and follow the route shown.

Take a taxi

The easiest solution, particularly if you're traveling as a family, but also the most expensive. Taxis charge 20% more between 10 p.m. and 5 a.m. A trip of about six miles (30 minutes) costs about ¥5,000.

NOTE!
Wait for the walk signal to cross the street, even at night.

HOW NOT TO MISS **THE LAST TRAIN**

The last trains usually leave between midnight and 1 a.m.

Try to get to the subway station before midnight (set an alarm on your phone). Even if you don't make your transfer, at least you'll be that much closer to your hotel.

Note the schedule of the last trains running to your hotel.

Credit: Orataw

IF YOUR HOTEL IS **FAR**

Capsule Hotel

Capsule hotels offer a pod equipped with a mattress and blanket, a light, and an electrical outlet. Bathrooms are shared. Depending on the district and amenities, one night costs between ¥2,500 and ¥6,000.

カプセルホテル

Capuseru hoteru

[cap-ou-sel-ou hotel-ou]

NOTE!
Most of these establishments are for salarymen working late and do not allow women.

Manga Café

A cross between a bookstore and an internet café, manga kissa let you rent a private booth (sometimes available for two) by the hour or in six- or twelve-hour increments. For about ¥2,000, you can:

- Lie down or even sleep on the mattress in the booth
- Surf the internet
- Browse thousands of manga (in Japanese)
- Use drink (or even ice cream!) machines for free
- Shower (if included with your package)

漫画喫茶

manga kissa

[mahn-gah keess-sah]

Karaoke

Turn lemons into lemonade and spend the entire night singing karaoke!

Ask for the shihatsu rate, which lets you stay until 5 a.m., around the time the trains start running again. You can get a private room (with couches you can nap on) and free access to a drink machine for about ¥1,500 to ¥2,000.

始発

shihatsu

[shee-hah-tsoo]

DEAD **BATTERIES**

A smartphone and pocket Wi-Fi device are an indispensable combo for any trip to Japan, so a dead battery can prove debilitating.

IF YOU DON'T HAVE **A CORD**

Electronics stores

Stores like Bic Camera, Yodobashi, and even Don Quijote have lockers for your phone. You can charge your device in 30 minutes for ¥100.

Mobile phone operators

Mobile phone operators like SoftBank and Docomo that sell phones offer phone lockers for free.

Karaoke bars and internet cafés

Book a session and then ask for a charger at the desk.

Solar-powered chargers

Tokyo has installed public chargers, labeled with a City Charge logo. Place your phone in one of the slots and let the sun do its work. It's not very effective on rainy days, though.

IF YOU HAVE **A CHARGER AND A CORD**

Cafés and fast-food restaurants

Most provide outlets only for paying customers, so you'll have to make a purchase.

Hotel lobbies

Outlets are usually available.

TIP!
Buy an extra power bank to avoid getting caught short.

Credit: Thomas Johnson

Credit: Stéfan

BUDDHIST TEMPLES
VS. SHINTO SHRINES

How to distinguish between these two types of sacred places, which have existed alongside each other in Japan for centuries.

Credit: 杉山宣嗣

Shinto is an animistic religion specific to Japan that worships thousands of divinities called kami. Shinto shrines are popular wedding venues.

Shinto shrine

神社

jinja
[jin-jah]

Buddhism is a monotheistic religion. Funerals are often held in Buddhist temples.

Buddhist temple

お寺

otera
[oh-tay-lah]

TIP!
Prayer offerings usually take the form of a five-yen coin, featuring a hole in the middle, for luck.

Clue 1: Name

Buddhist temples end in -tera (or -dera), -ji, or -in.

Most Shinto shrines end in -jingu.

Clue 2: Entrance

Shinto shrines feature a huge torii gate at the entrance. Bow before you pass through and keep to the sides of the pathway. The middle is reserved for the divinities.

Clue 3: Purification ritual

At Buddhist temples, visitors purify themselves with incense smoke before entering.

At Shinto shrines, you purify yourself with water as follows:

Use the ladle to pour water on your left hand.

Switch hands and pour water on your right hand.

Switch again. Cup your left palm and pour water into it.

Use this water to cleanse your mouth. Spit it out next to the tub of water.

Rinse your left hand again.

Let water run down the ladle handle to cleanse it before replacing the ladle for the next person.

Clue 4: Architecture

At Buddhist temples, the roofs are frequently made of tiles. There are multiple buildings and very often a pagoda. There is usually a Buddha statue in the main building.

Shinto shrines are usually divided into two buildings. One houses the divinity, and the main building is for prayer. Sometimes you'll see statues of animals.

Clue 5: Prayers

At Buddhist temples, praying is done in silence after presenting an offering and bowing.

At Shinto shrines, an offering is given, followed by the ringing of a bell, two bows, two claps of the hands, and a final long bow during which the prayer is uttered.

Credit: RachelH_

MAILING
POSTCARDS

Sending a postcard is so much more meaningful in the age of social media. But it's not always a simple task in Tokyo!

WHERE TO FIND POSTCARDS

The Japanese don't typically send postcards. Instead, they have a custom of bringing home souvenirs for friends and family. As a result, gift shops often sell trinkets but rarely postcards.

Check out stationery shops, 100-yen shops, and post offices. Post offices in particular sell permanent and seasonal collections of postcards. Plus, you can buy stamps at the same time.

Postcard
はがき
hagaki
[ha-gah-kee]

WHERE TO FIND STAMPS

The international rate for a standard postcard is:

¥70 without an envelope

¥110 with an envelope

You can buy stamps at konbini, but post offices are better because you can ask for decorative stamps.

Stamp
切手
kitte
[kee-tay]

Decorative stamp
きれいな切手
kireina kitte
[kee-ray-nah kee-tay]

NOTE!
Remember to include the country in the address on the card, as well as the words AIRMAIL.

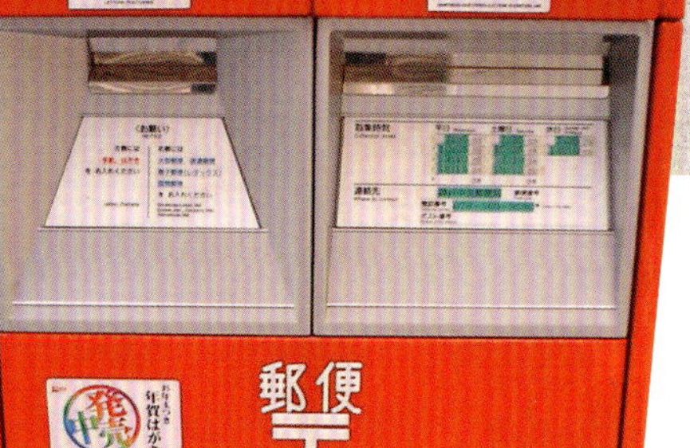

SENDING YOUR POSTCARD

Japanese mailboxes have two slots. Insert your postcard into the one on the left.

RETURNING HOME

All good things must come to an end. Here are a few final tips to make the trip home as smooth as possible.

SUITCASES

Check to see how many checked bags (one or two) per person your airline allows.

Weigh your bags. Weight limits also vary by airline.

If your bags are too heavy, mail the heaviest items to yourself. Packages have a 66-lb (30-kg) weight limit.

You have four mailing options. Choose one of the cheaper ones.

Service	Express Mail Service	Airmail	Surface Air Lifted	Surface (Sea Mail)
Duration	2–4 days	3–6 days	1–2 weeks	1–2 months

I want to send a package to the USA

アメリカに荷物を送りたいです

Amerika ni nimotsu wo okuritai desu
[Ah-meh-ri-kah nee nee-moh-tsoo oh oh-koo-lee-ty dess]

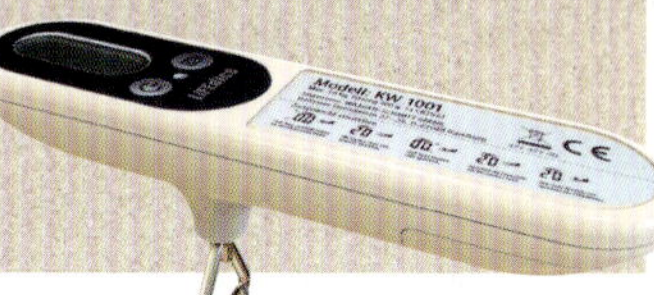

Credit: Lifedics

TIP!
The day before you leave, have a takkyūbin (see p. 20) deliver your bags to the airport so you don't have to carry them with you.

NOTE!
Avoid rush hour (7 a.m.–9 a.m. and 6 p.m.–8 p.m.), especially if you have a lot of bags.

TIP!
Invest in an electronic luggage scale, available at any electronics store.

Credit: Tokyo convention and visitor bureau

AT THE **AIRPORT**

Place your pocket Wi-Fi device, accessories, and case in the envelope it came with, seal it, and slip it into the mailbox in the lobby.

NOTE!
There are no mailboxes past security in the international area!

Spend the last few yen on your IC Card at a shop or konbini.

BACK HOME

NOTE!
Keep an eye on your belongings. Not every city is as safe as Tokyo!

You might find yourself standing to the left on escalators and moving walkways. And depending on how long you were away, it may take a few hours to a few days to get used to the lack of konbini or people saying "Sumimasen!"

On the other hand, now that you've seen the benefits of the Japanese belief in patience, try to apply it back home when you're in crowds, long lines, or traffic jams.

APPENDICES

TOKYO SUBWAY MAP

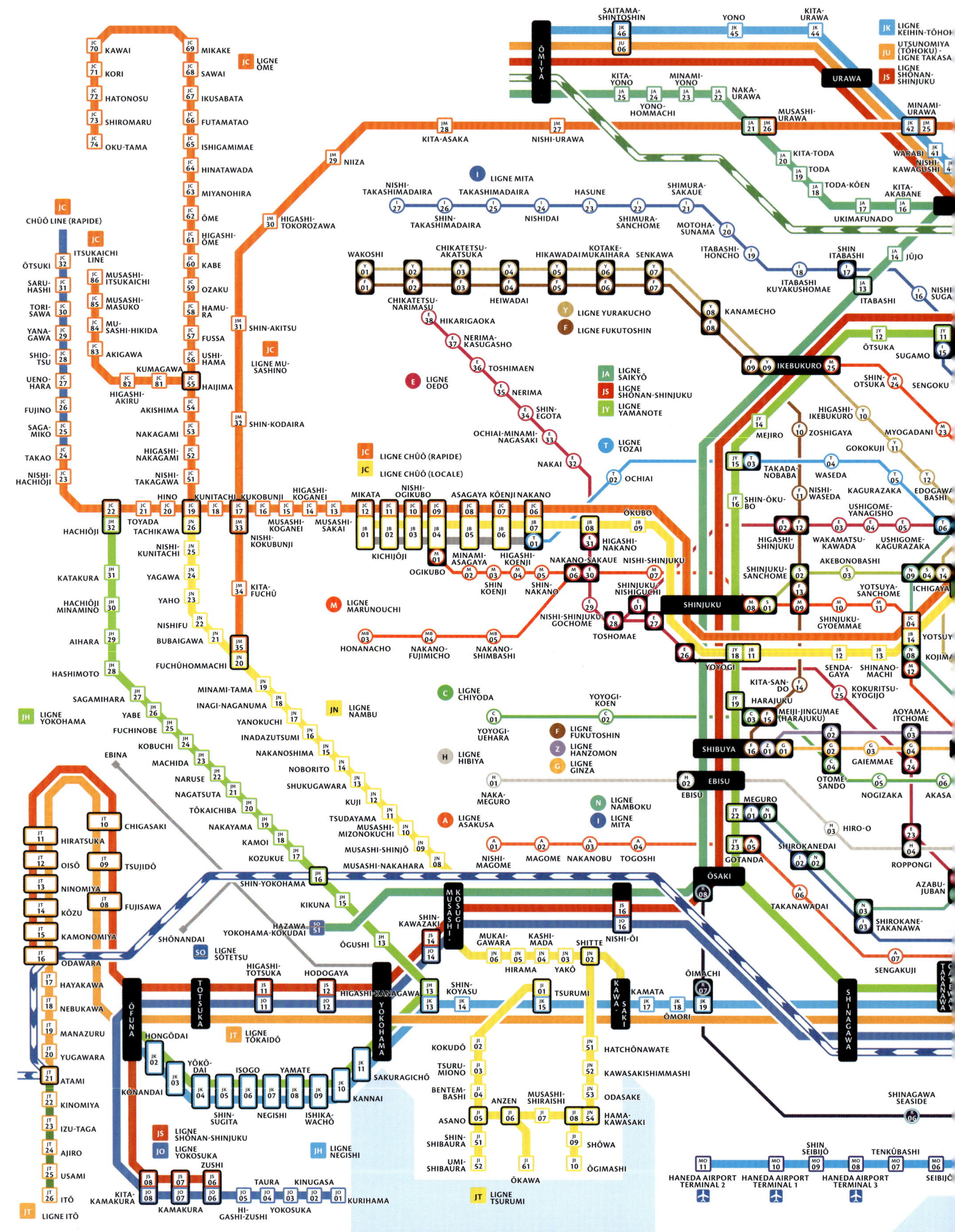

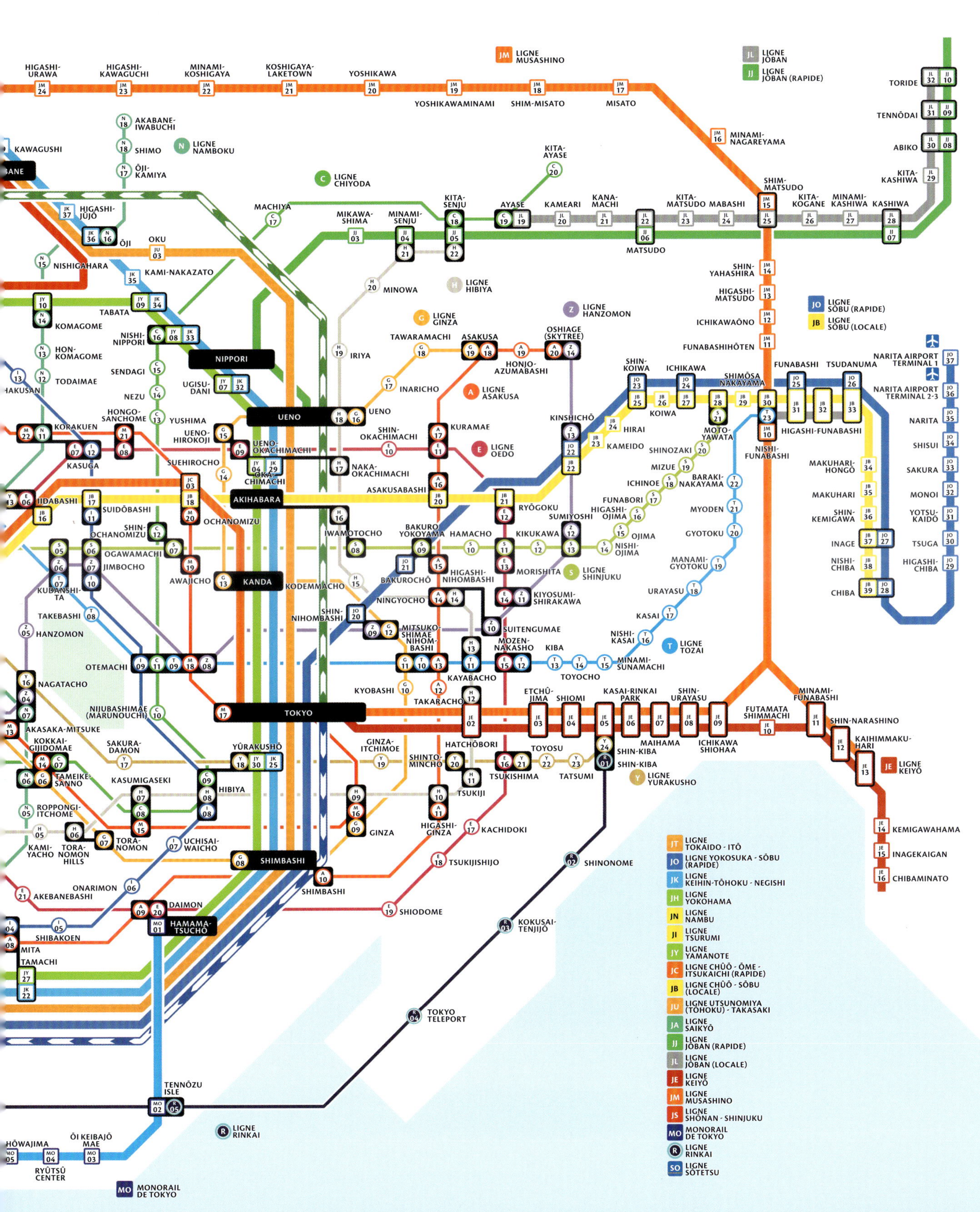
JM LIGNE MUSASHINO
JL LIGNE JOBAN
JJ LIGNE JOBAN (RAPIDE)
N LIGNE NAMBOKU
C LIGNE CHIYODA
JO LIGNE SOBU (RAPIDE)
JB LIGNE SOBU (LOCALE)
H LIGNE HIBIYA
G LIGNE GINZA
Z LIGNE HANZOMON
A LIGNE ASAKUSA
E LIGNE OEDO
S LIGNE SHINJUKU
T LIGNE TOZAI
Y LIGNE YURAKUSHO
JE LIGNE KEIYO

HIGASHI-URAWA
HIGASHI-KAWAGUCHI
MINAMI-KOSHIGAYA
KOSHIGAYA-LAKETOWN
YOSHIKAWA
YOSHIKAWAMINAMI
SHIM-MISATO
MISATO
MINAMI-NAGAREYAMA
SHIN-YAHASHIRA
HIGASHI-MATSUDO
ICHIKAWAONO
FUNABASHIHOTEN
TORIDE
TENNODAI
ABIKO
KITA-KASHIWA
SHIM-MATSUDO
KITA-KOGANE
MINAMI-KASHIWA
KASHIWA
MATSUDO
MABASHI
KITA-MATSUDO
KITA-SENJU
AYASE
KAMEARI
KANA-MACHI
KITA-AYASE
AKABANE-IWABUCHI
SHIMO
OJI-KAMIYA
KAWAGUSHI
BANE
HIGASHI-JUJO
OJI
OKU
NISHIGAHARA
KAMI-NAKAZATO
MACHIYA
MIKAWA-SHIMA
MINAMI-SENJU
MINOWA
IRIYA
TAWARAMACHI
ASAKUSA
OSHIAGE (SKYTREE)
HONJO-AZUMABASHI
SHIN-KOIWA
ICHIKAWA
SHIMOSA-NAKAYAMA
FUNABASHI
TSUDANUMA
NARITA AIRPORT TERMINAL 1
NARITA AIRPORT TERMINAL 2-3
NARITA
SHISUI
SAKURA
MONOI
YOTSU-KAIDO
TSUGA
HIGASHI-CHIBA
NISHI-CHIBA
INAGE
CHIBA
SHIN-KEMIGAWA
MAKUHARI
MAKUHARI-HONGO
HIGASHI-FUNABASHI
NISHI-FUNABASHI
MOTO-YAWATA
KOIWA
KINSHICHO
HIRAI
KAMEIDO
SHINOZAKI
MIZUE
ICHINOE
FUNABORI
HIGASHI-OJIMA
OJIMA
NISHI-OJIMA
BARAKI-NAKAYAMA
MYODEN
GYOTOKU
MANAMI-GYOTOKU
URAYASU
KASAI
NISHI-KASAI
TABATA
KOMAGOME
NISHI-NIPPORI
NIPPORI
SENDAGI
NEZU
UGISU-DANI
UENO
YUSHIMA
UENO-HIROKOJI
UENO-OKACHIMACHI
OKACHIMACHI
SHIN-OKACHIMACHI
NAKA-OKACHIMACHI
KURAMAE
ASAKUSABASHI
HON-KOMAGOME
TODAIMAE
HAKUSAN
NEZU
HONGO-SANCHOME
KORAKUEN
KASUGA
SUEHIROCHO
IIDABASHI
SUIDOBASHI
SHIN-OCHANOMIZU
OCHANOMIZU
AKIHABARA
IWAMOTOCHO
BAKURO-YOKOYAMA
HAMACHO
KIKUKAWA
SUMIYOSHI
RYOGOKU
OGAWAMACHI
JIMBOCHO
AWAJICHO
KANDA
KODEMMACHO
BAKUROCHO
HIGASHI-NIHOMBASHI
NINGYOCHO
KIYOSUMI-SHIRAKAWA
MORISHITA
KUBANSHI-TA
TAKEBASHI
HANZOMON
SHIN-NIHOMBASHI
SUITENGUMEA
MITSUKO-SHIMAE-NIHOM-BASHI
MOZEN-NAKASHO
KIBA
MINAMI-SUNAMACHI
TOYOCHO
KASAI-RINKAI PARK
OTEMACHI
KYOBASHI
KAYABACHO
NAGATACHO
NIJUBASHIMAE (MARUNOUCHI)
TOKYO
TAKARACHO
ETCHU-JIMA
SHIOMI
SHIN-URAYASU
MAIHAMA
ICHIKAWA SHIOHAA
FUTAMATA SHIMMACHI
MINAMI-FUNABASHI
SHIN-NARASHINO
KAIHIMMAKU-HARI
AKASAKA-MITSUKE
KOKKAI-GIJIDOMAE
SAKURA-DAMON
KASUMIGASEKI
HIBIYA
GINZA-ITCHIMOE
YURAKUSHO
SHINTO-MINCHO
HATCHOBORI
TOYOSU
TSUKISHIMA
TSUKIJI
HIGASHI-GINZA
KACHIDOKI
TATSUMI
SHIN-KIBA
SHINONOME
TAMEIKE-SANNO
ROPPONGI-ITCHOME
TORA-NOMON
UCHISAI-WAICHO
GINZA
TSUKIJISHIJO
KOKUSAI-TENJIJO
KAMI-YACHO
TORA-NOMON HILLS
SHIMBASHI
SHIODOME
ONARIMON
AKEBANEBASHI
DAIMON
HAMAMA-TSUCHO
SHIBAKOEN
MITA
TAMACHI
TOKYO TELEPORT
TENNOZU ISLE
HOWAJIMA
OI KEIBAJO MAE
RYUTSU CENTER
KEMIGAWAHAMA
INAGEKAIGAN
CHIBAMINATO

IT LIGNE TOKAIDO - ITO
JO LIGNE YOKOSUKA - SOBU (RAPIDE)
JK LIGNE KEIHIN-TOHOKU - NEGISHI
JH LIGNE YOKOHAMA
JN LIGNE NAMBU
JI LIGNE TSURUMI
JY LIGNE YAMANOTE
JC LIGNE CHUO - OME - ITSUKAICHI (RAPIDE)
JB LIGNE CHUO - SOBU (LOCALE)
JU LIGNE UTSUNOMIYA (TOHOKU) - TAKASAKI
JA LIGNE SAIKYO
JJ LIGNE JOBAN (RAPIDE)
JL LIGNE JOBAN (LOCALE)
JE LIGNE KEIYO
JM LIGNE MUSASHINO
JS LIGNE SHONAN - SHINJUKU
MO MONORAIL DE TOKYO
R LIGNE RINKAI
SO LIGNE SOTETSU
MONORAIL DE TOKYO

HIRAGANA

あ	a	い	i	う	u	え	e	お	o
か	ka	き	ki	く	ku	け	ke	こ	ko
さ	sa	し	shi	す	su	せ	se	そ	so
た	ta	ち	chi	つ	tsu	て	te	と	to
な	na	に	ni	ぬ	nu	ね	ne	の	no
は	ha	ひ	hi	ふ	fu	へ	he	ほ	ho
ま	ma	み	mi	む	mu	め	me	も	mo
や	ya			ゆ	yu			よ	yo
ら	ra	り	ri	る	ru	れ	re	ろ	ro
わ	wa							を	wo
								ん	-n
が	ga	ぎ	gi	ぐ	gu	げ	ge	ご	go
ざ	za	じ	ji	ず	zu	ぜ	ze	ぞ	zo
だ	da	ぢ	ji	づ	zu	で	de	ど	do
ば	ba	び	bi	ぶ	bu	べ	be	ぼ	bo
ぱ	pa	ぴ	pi	ぷ	pu	ぺ	pe	ぽ	po

KATAKANA

ア	a	イ	i	ウ	u	エ	e	オ	o
カ	ka	キ	ki	ク	ku	ケ	ke	コ	ko
サ	sa	シ	shi	ス	su	セ	se	ソ	so
タ	ta	チ	chi	ツ	tsu	テ	te	ト	to
ナ	na	ニ	ni	ヌ	nu	ネ	ne	ノ	no
ハ	ha	ヒ	hi	フ	fu	ヘ	he	ホ	ho
マ	ma	ミ	mi	ム	mu	メ	me	モ	mo
ヤ	ya			ユ	yu			ヨ	yo
ラ	ra	リ	ri	ル	ru	レ	re	ロ	ro
ワ	wa							ヲ	wo
								ン	-n
ガ	ga	ギ	gi	グ	gu	ゲ	ge	ゴ	go
ザ	za	ジ	ji	ズ	zu	ゼ	ze	ゾ	zo
ダ	da	ヂ	ji	ヅ	zu	デ	de	ド	do
バ	ba	ビ	bi	ブ	bu	ベ	be	ボ	bo
パ	pa	ピ	pi	プ	pu	ペ	pe	ポ	po

NOTES & **IDEAS**

NOTES & **IDEAS**

NOTES & IDEAS